TRIALS AND TRIUMPHS OF FAITH

MARY COLE

Finally, my brethren, be strong in the Lord, and in the power of his might. Put on the whole armor of God, that ye may be able to stand against the wiles of the devil. - Paul.

1st WORLD
LIBRARY
Literary Society

Trials and Triumphs of Faith

Mary Cole

© 1st World Library – Literary Society, 2004
PO Box 2211
Fairfield, IA 52556
www.1stworldlibrary.org
First Edition

LCCN: 2004091262

Softcover ISBN: 1-59540-680-8
eBook ISBN: 1-59540-780-4

Purchase *"Trials and Triumphs of Faith"*
as a traditional bound book at:
www.1stWorldLibrary.org/purchase.asp?ISBN=1-59540-680-8

1st World Library Literary Society is a nonprofit
organization dedicated to promoting literacy by:

- Creating a free internet library accessible from any
  computer worldwide.
- Hosting writing competitions and offering book
  publishing scholarships.

Readers interested in supporting literacy
through sponsorship, donations or
membership please contact:
literacy@1stworldlibrary.org
Check us out at: www.1stworldlibrary.org

CONTENTS

POEMS

PREFACE

The history of the world consists mainly of the stories of the lives of certain men and women whose deeds have been of sufficient importance to make them worth relating. The lives of some persons have been worth narrating because of their abounding in deeds of great merit, such as the lives of Washington, Gladstone, Frances E. Willard, and Joan of Arc. The lives of others have been thought worth narrating because of their great wickedness, as the lives of Nero and Queen Mary of England.

But the church too has a history. This history differs from the history of the world, in that it does not record merely the doings of man, but the workings of God through man as his instruments. God is a jealous God who manifests himself only through those who are willing to give him all the glory. Hence not many names of the wise, powerful, talented men of the earth have been enrolled on the history of the church, since they were not humble enough to submit fully into God's hands. In the church truly this scripture has been proved: "God has used the weak things of the world to confound the mighty."

Sister Mary Cole, of whose life this book is a brief, authentic sketch, had a natural inheritance that seemed calculated to shut her forever out of a place in the history of the world or of the church. Born with a body that from her earliest childhood was racked with pain, deprived by ill health of education, she seemed naturally unfitted to fill any place in the world and doomed to be only a burden to herself and her friends. How God took her, healed her, and fitted her for his service, and how he used her as an instrument for his glory, is the story of her life.

The publication of the story of her life was so remote from her thoughts that it was only by the solicitation of some one who had been greatly helped by her faith and experience and the workings of God through her, and who was unwilling that her trials and triumphs should be lost as a part of the history of the church, that she was prevailed upon to write this brief narrative of her life and work. The story of her life would not, indeed, be worth telling were it stripped of the manifestations of God's power. As you read this simple story, you will see clearly that, as Sister Cole has herself expressed so many times, what she is she is by God's grace, and that all she has accomplished she has accomplished through God's power. If you will take at their value the oft-repeated expressions, "God told me," "God spoke to me," "God made me to understand," realizing that these words tell us something that actually happened, you will get some idea of how marvelously God can use even the weakest members of the human race.

Aside from the interest this brief history will have for those readers who have had the pleasure of a personal acquaintance with Sister Cole and who have had the privilege of listening to her stirring messages delivered under the anointing of God's Spirit, it can not fail to interest and profit all who take pleasure in reading about the dealings of God with man.

It is the sincere wish of the author and of all those who had a hand in preparing this work, that it will show some their greater privileges in the kingdom of God, and that it will help some to covet the divine help, guidance, and power that are the heritage of all God's children.

J.W.P.

Chapter I

Birth and Ancestry

Like many other people of European descent, born in this country, I can trace my ancestry back to their emigration from Europe; but being so far removed from European environment, my nationality can best be expressed by the short but comprehensive term, American.

My father was born in Hunterdon County, New Jersey. He was a descendant of the German Hessians who were brought to this country by the English to fight against the Americans in the Revolutionary War. It is said that from his mother's side he inherited a small portion of Turkish blood. Father's childhood days were spent near some of the Revolutionary battle-fields, where he played with cannon balls that had been used during that great struggle. Perhaps his early surroundings may have developed in him the spirit of partiotism that manifested itself later when, during the Civil War, he stood by his country and defended the stars and stripes.

My mother was born in Ohio near the Pennsylvania border, but was reared in Carroll County, Ohio.

Her father, whose name was Fleming, was of

Scotch-Irish descent. His ancestors came from Ireland at an early day and settled first in Pennsylvania, and later in Ohio. When Mother's great-grandfather and his cousin came over from Ireland and landed in New York, they heard a parrot talking. It said, "A beggar and a clodhopper; a beggar and a clodhopper." They had never heard of a parrot before. The great-grandfather said to his cousin, "Pat, Pat, what kind of a world have we got into? Aven the burds of the woods are making fun of us."

My mother's mother was of German descent, and could speak the German language; but she died when mother was but a small child. Very soon afterward Mother's father married an Irish lady by the name of Margret Potter. Mother's stepmother took her drams, had dances, etc.; but Mother was spiritually inclined. In her eighteenth year while attending a Methodist meeting, she was convicted of her sins. She was not saved at the meeting, but prayed through by herself to an experience. God revealed himself to her in a marvelous way and gave her the witness that she was born of him.

Mother's father was a Universalist until after she was grown. At that time, although he had never professed a change of heart, he joined the Christian church. Mother's steady Christian character was, therefore, developed without human encouragement; she got help from no one but God. Her older sister said to her one day, "Rebecca, our dear mother died a Universalist; are you going to forsake her faith?" Mother answered, "If Mother did the best she knew, that is between her and her God; it is my duty to do the best I know." Later this sister joined the Catholic Church and finally died in the Catholic home for widows.

I was born August 23, 1853, the seventh of a family of twelve children - eight sons and four daughters. Two died before the last two were born, so that there were never more than ten of us living at the same time.

The oldest child was Jeremiah. Mother said that at his birth she gave him to the Lord, and prayed earnestly that God would make him like Jeremiah of old. God chose him for the ministry, and he died triumphant in the faith. He discerned the one body, the church, from the time the truth of the unity of God's people was first preached. His body lies in the cemetery near Hammond, Louisiana.

The second child was John. He enlisted in the army and gave his life for his country. Out of this family of twelve children, God chose three for the ministry: one of these has gone to his reward and the other two remain to work for the Master.

At the time of my birth, my parents lived on a farm adjoining the town of Decatur, in the State of Iowa. Later the town was enlarged until it included Father's farm, which was sold for town lots. My parents remained in Iowa until I was a year old, and then moved to Illinois, where they remained for two years. When I was three years old, they settled in Pettis County, Missouri, near the town of Belmont, afterwards called Windsor. It was there that I spent my childhood and the years of my young womanhood.

Chapter II

Early Afflictions

"Misery stole me at my birth
And cast me helpless on the wild."

The words of this hymn express my condition from my first advent into the world. My mother had overworked before I was born; and, as a result, I suffered bodily affliction from infancy. I was scarely two years old when I began having spasms. My eyes would roll back in my head, I would froth at the mouth, the tendons of my jaws would draw, causing me to bite my cheeks until the blood ran from my mouth, and I would become unconscious. Although I would remain unconscious for only a short time, yet while I lay in that condition I seemed as one dead. Upon regaining consciousness, I seemed dazed all the rest of that day; and not until I had had a night's sleep, did I have a clear perception of what was going on around me. Sometimes two or three days would pass before I was fully restored.

I hada number of these spansm when I was too young to know anything about them. The first one of which I remember, I begain to turn blind and did not know what was the matter; but I soon learned the nature of my affliction. I had to be very careful what I did. If I exposed myself to the direct rays of the sun or even looked straight at the sun, I was likely to have a spasm; if I drank sweet milk it was likely to have the same result.

When I quit school at the age of ten years and had nothing to occupy my mind, my thoughts centered on my suffering and the frequency of my spasms seemed to increase. After having a spasm my mind was greatly afflicted with melancholy and depression. I dreaded the recurrence of the fits, and looked forward to their coming with such abhorrence that often the fear of having a spasm would bring on the very thing I dreaded.

From the time I can first recollect, most of my life was spent in sadness and disappointment. It seemed as if my whole being were a mass of suffering and affliction. The doctor said there was nothing sound about me but my lungs. Most of my time I appeared to be nothing but a voice. So far as I remember, not one day of that period of my life was passed without pain and suffering. My high temper, of course, added mental suffering to the physical.

Many times I wondered why I could not die. My suffering was greatly increased by melancholy and mental depression. I often sat beside my mother and cried, "Mother, why can't I die? Why did I not die when I was a child? I am a trial to myself and to all around me." Mother would say, "Mary, God has a bright design in all this. We do not know the reason why you are so afflicted, but we will know sometime." With such comforting words she many times soothed my troubled spirit. God blessed me with a dear Christian mother. Her gentle, patient life - so loving and Christlike - stamped upon my soul in early childhood the ideal of real Christian character. I had before me constantly an example of what I ought to be. As I look back at those days, my association with my mother seems to have been the only bright spot in my early life.

At six years of age I began to have dyspepsia, and as a result, could eat but very little food without suffering. Up to this time and later, I could walk a mile or more; but was liable at any time to have a fit. When about twelve or thirteen years of age, other afflictions set in, such as spinal and female trouble.

In my fifteenth year I became a helpless invalid, and lay in bed for five months at one time. When I first became helpless, I thought I was dying. I knew if I went into eternity as I then was I would be lost, and suffered terrible mental anguish. My dear mother came to my bedside with comforting words: "Mary, put your trust in the Lord." I could move neither hand nor foot but could only say, "Mother, I am trying to," knowing at the same time that I was not capable of meeting the conditions - repentance, etc., I decided that I would not tell Mother nor any one else that I felt that I was lost, even if I died in that condition; but God in his mercy saw fit to lengthen out my life.

Viewed from the standpoint of mature life, those early years remind me of the experience of the Israel-ites when they came to Marah, where the waters were bitter, and where Moses put something into the bitter waters to make them sweet. In my unsaved condition, I was at Marah; but when the Lord saved my soul, he put something into the bitter stream of my life that made it sweet, and I can truly say, "My December is as pleasant as May: my summer lasts all the year." Yes, I can now obey God's Word: "Rejoice evermore; pray without ceasing; and in everything give thanks" (1 Thessalonians 5:14-16). Oh, what a wonderful change God wrought! It is all through grace divine; for the promise is, "All things work together for good to them that love God."

Chapter III

Incidents of Childhood

The old home farm near Windsor, Missouri, where I spent my childhood and early womanhood, was heavily timbered on the west and the south. There was also a good-sized apple orchard north of the house and a number of beautiful shade trees in the yard, which gave the place a homelike appearance. The house was very ordinary - just a large front room, a large bedroom, an attic large enough for three or four beds, and a large log kitchen.

In those days, and even until long after the Civil War, the houses were lighted mostly by candles. The old-fashioned fireplace gave us both light and heat in the rooms where they were, and made very pleasant the long winter evenings. Of course, in many ways they were not equal to our modern improvements, but we had some very happy times around the old fireplace. Mother made the candles we used, in molds especially designed for that purpose. I will not soon forget how I used to watch her put in the cotton wick, tie it at a certain place, and then melt and pour in the tallow. As soon as the tallow cooled, we had candles. Sometimes when we had no candles, we used what was called a grease lamp. This was merely a saucer with a little grease in it and a twisted rag, the greater part of which lay in the grease in the bottom of the saucer. The end which extended up over the edge of the saucer was lighted, and this device served as a lamp until Mother could make more candles.

Near the house was a garden from which Mother used often to gather bouquets to cheer me in my lonely hours. These loving acts of Mother's meant much to me in my affliction. Jesus said that the gift of a cup of cold water will be rewarded. I am sure that Mother's reward will be great.

When I was about five or six years old, an incident occurred which shows that I, although greatly afflicted, was not altogether wanting in activity. Two of my older sisters and I were playing on a shed adjoining one side of the corn-crib. My sisters wanted to jump off the shed, but were a little afraid to do so for fear they would hurt themselves. They finally decided that they would have me jump first, and if it did not hurt me, then they would jump. Little as I was, I understood their scheme. Nevertheless, I jumped. It hurt me quite a little; but when they asked me if I was hurt, I said, "No." Thinking then, that it would not hurt them, they jumped but they were considerably hurt too. Again they asked if it hurt me, and I admitted that it had. "Why did you not tell us?" "Because," I replied, "you were playing off on me because I am the youngest, and I would not let you know, so that you would have a chance to get hurt too."

One morning when I was about six years old, I was going to school in company with my brothers and sisters and other children who went the same road. It was late in the fall, and a heavy rain that had recently fallen, made the narrow lane through which we were obliged to pass, very muddy. Cattle had made deep tracks in the mud, in which the water had collected and then frozen. The bubbles underneath the ice had the appearance of money, and we children ran along looking at the bubbles, and saying "I have found some money." All at once I was sure that I did see a real coin under the ice at the bottom of one of the holes. When I called out "I have found some money," my brothers came quickly to investigate; and, sure enough, there was a fifty-cent piece stuck to the rim of an old pocket book. It had lain there so long that the leather had all rotted away. I was so delighted and spent so much time in enjoying the treasure I had found that I learned but very little that day.

One of my earliest recollections is of committing these lines to memory:

"In His pure eyes it is a sin To steal a penny or a pin."

Not long after this, when I was about four years old, I think, I went with my oldest sister to one of our neighbors on an errand. My sister, who could weave, wanted me to go to the home of another neighbor near by to borrow a part for the old-fashioned loom she was using. While at the house I saw a piece of pink calico about an inch square that attracted my childish fancy. I thought how nice it would be for the little quilt I had begun to piece. As I had no pocket, I put the piece of calico into the bosom of my dress and went back to my sister holding it as if I feared it would get away.

Noticing what I was doing, she said, "Mary, what is the matter?" "Nothing," I answered. "What have you there?" "Nothing," I replied again. Right there I told two falsehoods, the first of which I had ever been guilty. They were like black spots on a white robe. My sister said, "I know you have something," and drew out my hand still grasping the scrap of calico. "Where did you get it?" I told the truth then, and she said that I must go back and tell the woman I had stolen it. She took me back; but she had to do all the talking.

The old lady wanted to excuse me, and said, "Oh, let her have it; it dosen't amount to anything"; but my sister said, "No, she shall not have it, for she did not ask for it." Oh, how awful I felt! It was about a mile to our house, and I cried nearly the whole way home. On the way I said, "Ell, don't tell Mother"; and she promised that she would not. I had experienced now what Paul meant when he said, "Sin revived and I died." It was the first time in my life I had ever known what guilt was. Reproof given at the first offense has saved me many temptations in later life. Only twice afterward do I remember of having had a like temptation.

Perhaps the influence of this incident was strengthened by a story that my mother related to me while I was still a child. This story made a deep impression upon my young heart. In Carroll County, Ohio, not far from where she was raised, there lived two families by the name of Long. The fathers were brothers. Two boys of the two families used to trap for mink and other fur-bearing animals during the winter season. As the fur of the mink at that time brought a good price, the boys were more anxious to catch mink than any other animal. One of the boys once found a mink in his cousin's trap. When he told his mother what he had seen, she said, "Go back, take the mink out of your cousin's trap, set the trap just as it was before, put the mink into your own trap, and tell your cousin that you have caught a mink; he will never know the difference."

The boy did as his mother advised, and the cousin never learned of the deception until many years later. The boy who had stolen the mink went from bad to worse until, during the outbreak of the Mormons, I think, he was implicated in the murder of Colonel Davenport of Iowa. While on the scaffold, he confessed that his first step downward was in taking the mink out of his cousin's trap and telling a falsehood about it. God's Word was verified: "For they have sown the wind, and they shall reap the whirlwind."

Parents, be careful what example you set before your children. If you set a wrong example, they may rise up and curse you: but if you teach them the good and right way, they will "rise up and call you blessed." If when parents see one of their children entering upon his first temptation to take things that do not belong to him, they would do their duty, there would be more honest children today. "Train up a child in the way he should go, and when he is old he will not depart from it."

From my earliest childhood I liked poetry and could readily commit it to memory. I often learned poems that were quite difficult for one of my age. The beautiful poems I learned were like rays of sunshine on my pathway and added much comfort to a life that had but few pleasures.

I learned the alphabet at home and so made quite rapid progress after I began attending school, although I was greatly hindered because of stammering. Some of my teachers were very helpful to me in overcoming this difficulty. When Mr. Nutter, who taught our school one winter, saw that I could not recite because of my impediment of speech, he had all the classes recite with me so as to take away the embarrassment. I felt very grateful for his kindness.

One day when I was ten years old, I had a fit at school. Father thought that while I was afflicted in this way, it would be hard on my mind for me to study, and it would be best to keep me at home. During my last term at school, I read in McGuffey's Fourth Reader, studied the second part of Arithmetic, had learned to spell fairly well in the old Elementary Speller, and had also begun geography - a study which I liked very much. I was beginning to learn to write; but as I was left-handed, my movements were very slow and awkward.

Chapter IV

Events During the War

I was eight years old when the Civil War began. The first event that I remember in connection with the war was our teacher's dismissing school one day so that we might go over to the public road to see the Union soldiers. I suppose there were at least a regiment of these troops, if not more. As I had never seen soldiers before, their fine appearance as they marched by, dressed in their uniforms, with their guns, bayonets, drums, and full military equipment, made a lasting impression on my childish mind.

At the beginning of the war, my father wished to move from the State where we were then living. Missouri was a slave State and he knew that there was trouble ahead. Perhaps father would have had his way, had not God shown mother in a dream that he would protect us, and that we would be as safe in Missouri as in any other place. Subsequent events proved that we did well to obey God, for none of our stock or property was taken. The deaths of my brother and sister were the most severe trials through which we had to pass.

In January, 1862, the Federal soldiers again came to our neighborhood and camped near the same place where I had first seen them; but, at this time, the scene excited in me entirely different emotions. Snow was on the ground; the weather was very cold; and the soldiers took rails and made a large bonfire to keep themselves warm. The sky was lit up with the flames, and to me, in my nervous condition, the scene was frightful.

That same evening some of the soldiers went down to our little town (then called Belmont, afterwards Windsor), brought back to the camp with them the hollow trunk of a tree containing a swarm of bees, and laid it down to take out the honey. Mrs. Hammond, the wife of our nearest neighbor on the east, who lived but a short distance from the camp, thinking that they were planting a cannon, became frightened and came over to our house with her two little children. She was afraid there was going to be a battle, and sought our house as a place of safety. She wanted to stay all night. Father pitied her; and in spite of the fact that the children were sick with diphtheria, he felt that he could not turn her out.

Thus we children were all exposed to diphtheria; and as my nerves were in such a bad condition, and as I was greatly frightened because of the news from the camp and the presence of the sick children, I was the first victim of the disease. The next to take it was my sister Katherine. Just before she took her bed, she got her feet wet, and therefore had the disease in a very malignant form. The doctor who was caring for her, assured us that she was better, but he told some of the neighbors that she could not live until morning. We did not know that she was seriously ill until Father, who was sitting up with her that night, said, "Katy, it's time to take your medicine." There was no answer; her gentle spirit had taken its flight.

The thought that my sister was dead was almost more than I could endure. The thought that she was gone into eternity, that I would never meet her again in this world, almost broke my heart. I wept for hours at a time. I would sit beside my mother weeping and wondering why my sister had been taken. It seemed that I could never forgive the doctor for deceiving us; and I think I never did fully forgive him, until the time when God pardoned my sins and gave me a forgiving spirit. Dear little sister Katherine! She was twelve years and six months old when she died. She was an unusual child - patient and kind - was never known to disobey her parents, and was loved by all.

The other members of the family took the diphtheria one by one, until all but my father and one brother had this awful disease. Some of us were sick for nearly two months and during this time none of the neighbors, except Daniel Douglas, our nearest neighbor on the west, came to lend any assistance. He came over and sat up a part of every other night when the sick ones were at their worst, and needed the most care. Even the woman who brought the disease to us refused to help, until she was compelled to do so by Mr. Douglas; and then she only helped to prepare Katherine's body for burial. It certainly was a sad time. Even nature seemed to cast a gloom over everything - much sleet fell, and everything had a dismal appearance.

It was during the war and sometime before Katherine's death that Mr. Hammond used to cross our orchard going to and from his work. One day Father said to one of the Hammond children, "Come over and get some apples to eat"; to which the child answered, "Oh, Papa brings us all the apples we want to eat. He gets them out of your orchard."

One day while my brother Harvey was passing through the orchard, he saw an apple caught in the fork of two limbs. Supposing that the apple had fallen from the tree and accidently lodged there, he ate it, and soon began to feel very sick. The doctor found upon examination that the boy was suffering from strychnine poisoning. From remarks that had been dropped, we thought we knew that a certain neighbor had poisoned the apple and that he had done it for spite. A visitor at our house remarked that she feared that the Union soldiers, who were then encamped near her home, would in their absence from home, get the strychnine they had bought for the rats and poison their meal or their water before they got home again. My brother suffered from the effects of the strychnine he had taken for a number of years before he fully recovered.

The husband of the woman of whom I have just spoken was a soldier in the Southern army. One time while he was out foraging, he went into a Union woman's house and asked for a pie. Finding out that she had her pies hidden under the puncheon floor, he raised a plank and proceeded to help himself. The woman, seeing her opportunity, threw the plank onto his neck and jumped on the plank. The man got a furlough, came home, and was confined to his bed for some time. It was reported about the neighborhood that he had a spell of fever.

The woman who brought the diphtheria to us sought our house as a place of refuge, because the house being "low and in a low place" the cannon balls would pass over it. After the Lord saved me, this incident came to my mind as a lesson in humility. "Low and in a low place." If we as God's servants keep humble and in a low place, the enemy may hurl his darts and shoot his cannon balls: they will go over us and will not harm us. If we don't want to be disturbed or crippled by the enemy of our souls, we should keep low at the feet of Jesus where he can continually shelter us. "He that dwelleth in the secret place of the most high, shall abide under the shadow of the Almighty."

Some time after these events the Southern soldiers, commonly known as "bushwhackers," came into our neighborhood and camped in the woods. One evening as it was growing dusk, my oldest sister and the one next older than I went after water to a well half way between our house and the house of our nearest neighbor on the west. From this well both families used water. The girls had to go down a steep hill to get to the well; and as they came back to the brow of the hill, they found our dog lying dead. While the girls were at the well, the soldiers had no doubt killed the dog with a club, as no one heard a gun fired. My sisters went home with the water and then went back to investigate; they wanted to be sure that it was our dog that had been killed. They heard men in the brush near the place where the dog was lying, and being very young and not realizing their danger, they talked rather loudly and boisterously, saying that if they could see the men in the brush, they would shoot them with their fingers. The crackling in the brush indicated that the men were very near.

That night a large number of these bushwhackers entered our neighbor's house and stole bonds, notes, and clothing estimated to be worth $2000. Mr. Douglas had just been to Sedalia, where he had procured a good supply of clothing. The soldiers pointed Mr. Douglas's own gun, which had never been known to miss fire before, at his head; but it failed to go off. Our house was not molested. The next day these same men caught one of Mr. Douglas's boys, made him take off his shoes, hat, and all his other clothing, except his underwear, and turned him loose. In this condition, he had to go about a quarter of a mile before reaching home.

It was probably some time after these events that the bushwhackers came to our house and wanted Mother to cook a meal for a dozen men. Mother was hardly able to be out of bed, but my sister Mehala, thinking that they were Union soldiers, said, "Mother, I can cook for them." "Well, Mehala," Mother said, "if you can, you may go ahead." Mother helped all she could. They baked two large pones of corn-bread in the oldfashioned fireplace and fried plenty of fresh beef. Although the soldiers had ordered food for a dozen men, only two of them came. One of them took the provisions and the other guarded the house until he thought we would have no chance to report them. Then they went to the home of a neighbor and with much bad language said that Mother was Union and therefore pretended to be sick and did not want to cook for them.

During the war, things we had to buy were very high and things we had to sell brought only a trifle. Father sold corn to the Union soldiers for 25 cents a bushel. In imagination I can see the government wagons coming to haul the corn away to their camp. The beds of the wagons were somewhat like those used today, only they sloped outward on either side until they would hold more than twice as much as our ordinary farm wagons.

At that time, flour cost $10.00 and upward, a barrel, calico from 35 to 45 cents a yard, and cotton yarn from

$9.00 to $11.00 a bunch. This quantity of yarn would make only about 25 yards of jeans. Mother did her own spinning and weaving until some years after the war. We sheared our own sheep, washed and picked the wool, and sent it to the carding machine, where it was made into rolls. Then Mother and my older sister, who was nearly grown, spun the yarn and wove it into jeans and linsey, and also into flannel and blankets. Mother made all the clothing for the family - underwear, pants, vests, coats, and even overcoats. I well remember the old loom and spinning wheel and the little wheel on which I used to quill for my sister while she wove. Small as I was, I had learned to knit. I knit mittens for the soldiers, for which I got 50 cents a pair at Sedalia, the nearest army post, twenty miles away.

In the early part of the war Father was a militiaman. At one time he came very near being accidently killed in his own orchard by some of his own men. Some Federal soldiers who were passing came into our orchard, and seeing Father at a distance, thought he was a Southerner. Father, seeing his danger, started to run; but one of the soldiers who was near enough to recognize him, cried, "Cole, don't run or they'll shoot you"; but Father thought he said, "Cole run or they'll shoot you." Finally they got him to understand what they meant, and his life was saved.

I am not sure how near to our home actual fighting occurred. There were no battles fought nearer than Lone Jack. A number of our neighbors, however, were shot down in their own dooryards by those of the other side. One of our neighbors who favored the South but who was willing to be anything for the sake of safety, got fooled three times in one day. When the Confederate soldiers came along, he thought they were

Federals and professed to be a Union man; and then when the Federal soldiers came by he thought they were Confederates and told them he favored the South. When his own men came by again, they took his property because he had lied to them. His wife followed the soldiers pleading, begging, and crying, until they gave up the property. In his case, lies did not prove to be a satisfactory refuge.

At Cole Camp, about twenty-five miles from our place lived some Germans - good honest people, who had worked hard and had gotten quite a bit of property together. These thrifty farmers were not disturbing either side, but some men around Windsor, who called themselves "Home Guards," went down to Cole Camp, killed these inoffensive Germans, stamped their heads with their boot-heels, took all of their goods that they could carry away, while the poor wives were begging for the lives of their companions. Then these miscreants returned to Windsor and divided the spoil. One of my brothers, a mere boy, who was working for one of the "Home Guards," overheard his employer quarreling with another man over the division of the booty.

Before the "Home Guards" started on this raid, a preacher named Pierce, of the M. E. South denomination, prayed for their success. After their return, my father overheard him and one of the raiders talking. Father overheard this man tell Pierce that his brother had killed nine Germans and stamped them on the head with his boot heel. Upon hearing this the preacher, throwing back his head, laughed heartily. He seemed to enjoy the story very much. Up until this time Father was a member of the M. E. South denomination; but after overhearing this conversation he no longer professed to be one of them. It has often been remarked that war makes men wicked; but Mother used to say that usually the wickedness was in the men already and that war merely gave them a chance to put their wickedness on exhibition. Boys, of course, were especially demoralized by soldier-life, coming in contact as they did with so many wicked influences.

In the early part of the war, both Father and my second brother, John, joined the militia, which was later disbanded. Before the war closed, Father reached his 45th year and after that was too old to go as a soldier. John was quite patriotic and wanted to enlist for regular service. Nevertheless, he and my oldest brother went to Illinois to attend school. When they started, Mother said, "John, don't enlist in the army any more." "Mother," he answered, "I won't unless they draft me; but if they draft I will volunteer, for I don't like the treatment of a drafted soldier."

Soon a rumor came that a draft was to be made, on purpose, I suppose, to "beat up" volunteers. So to avoid being drafted, my brother volunteered. He had been exposed to the measles shortly before his enlistment, but supposed that when he joined the army he would get a furlough for at least twenty days. He was disappointed: next day they got marching orders. He took the measles, had to go out on duty when not able, took cold, and soon died with congestion of the lungs. His body lies in the soldiers' graveyard at Chattanooga, Tenn.

About the year 1894, I think, while my youngest brother and I were out in gospel work, the Lord greatly burdened my heart to pray for Mother's support. My brother and I were supposed to help provide for her;

and at this time Mother was especially in need, although I did not know it. The Lord showed me that I should save up what I had on hands for Mother's support until I should reach home, and that if I did not I would feel very sorry.

I did as God directed. When I reached home, Mother began to tell me of the poor crops and other drawbacks and what a hard time they had had. I told her I was glad to see that she had salvation, even if she did not have much of this world's goods, for I had seen many people with much of this world's goods, but with no experience of salvation, and they were in worse condition than she. I was still burdened to pray the Lord to supply Mother's needs; not only for the present, but while she lived.

When, after about three weeks' visit at home, I started again in the gospel work, I gave Mother all the change I had to spare. As I did so, she looked at me with tears running down her cheeks and said, "Mary, I don't want to take this; the cause needs it so badly." "Mother," I said, "you are a part of the cause." She laughed and cried but took the money. Shortly after this I got a postal card from my brother at home, saying that he had news from Washington, that Mother had been granted a pension because of my brother John's death during the Civil War. For three years she had been trying to get this pension and had about given up hope of ever receiving it. Mother received $400.00 back pension and $12.00 a month for the remainder of her life. The Lord showed me that my prayer was answered for Mother's support, and the burden left me.

Chapter V

Conversion and Sanctification

A few years after I became a helpless invalid, I was somewhat wrought upon by the Spirit of God, but had no advice as to what I should do. I joined the M. E. Church on probation, although I was yet unsaved. The minister who received me into the church, did not inquire whether I was saved or not, nor did he ask about my spiritual welfare.

In my nineteenth year I was convicted of my sins, after the following circumstance: I was having a quarrel with one of my younger brothers. We were both high-spirited and each wanted to have his own way. While the quarrel was in progress, Mother came on the scene, and what she heard was enough to make her heart ache. "Mary, why don't you set a better example?" "Mother," I said, "he commenced on me first. If you make him behave himself, I will behave." "Mary, I am afraid you children will never stop your quarreling until you land in perdition; and if I were out of the way, you would soon be there. You act just as if you wanted me out of the way." I saw her standing there as pale as a corpse with the big tears rolling down her face. She was always pale in those days. I said, "Mother, don't break my heart." "Mary," said she, "you broke my heart first." "Mother, won't you forgive me?"

"Yes," she answered, "I forgive you; but there is one higher than I whom you have offended, and you will have to ask his forgiveness."

Up to that time I was not under conviction, but the Lord now began to answer the prayer of my oldest brother, who had been praying for my conviction. That same evening I went into the garden, and earnestly asked the Lord to convict me of my sins. I remember now that he had convicted me in the past but that I had resisted until conviction left me. I said to the Lord, "I will not fight conviction now if it kills me right on the spot." The Lord took me at my word; he knew I meant what I said with all my heart. I arose from my knees, and walked toward the house, with such a deep realization of God's displeasure on my lost soul that it seemed as if the earth would open and swallow me up. I shall never forget that awful experience. I think I fully comprehended God's displeasure against rebellious souls, but in his wrath he remembered mercy, and I found myself seeking God with all my heart. I could not weep, but my heart was sincere and deeply determined to seek God until I should know that I was saved.

I did not find the Lord at once and the enemy brought discouragement against my soul. I was just about to come to the conclusion that I would seek God only a week, and that if I did not find him then I would quit. But as I walked through the front room, I noticed an old Methodist hymn-book lying on the stand. I opened it and as God would have it, my eyes fell on these lines: "And will you basely to the tempter yield?" Going to the kitchen where Mother was washing, I said, "Mother, there is a hymn in this book that ought to be torn out." She said, "Why, Mary?" After I had read the line to her she said, "Mary, can't you adopt the next line as yours? 'No, in the strength of Jesus, no, I never will give up my shield.'" I decided then and there to seek God until the day of my death, or until I found him.

My oldest brother and I went to prayer. He asked me to pray, but all I have ever remembered saying is, "Lord have mercy on me. Lord hear me." He said, "Mary, the Lord does have mercy on you and the Lord does hear you, or you could not have prayed as you have been praying." He asked me whether I was willing to live or die for the Lord; and I said, "I am willing to live, but I am not willing to die in this condition," He replied, "All the Lord wants is your will. He will not let you die in this condition when you want to get saved." But I still persisted that I wasn't willing to die in that condition.

Then the enemy tried to bring confusion upon me. The burden of my guilt was all gone and the devil suggested that I was worse than I had thought, that my heart was so hard I could not mourn for my sins any more. Howbeit, the dear Lord came to my rescue. He reminded me that my repentance was genuine, and therefore accepted by him; and that all he required of me was to exercise faith in his promises, and that if I could not do that immediately, I could begin to quote his word, "Lord, I believe; help thou my unbelief." I kept repeating that declaration and prayer all day long and until late in the afternoon.

I got hold of a little tract in which God's promises were simplified; for instance, "He is our light in darkness; our wisdom in ignorance; our counsellor in perplexity." I said, "Lord, I am perplexed: the burden of guilt is gone and I can't mourn any more, but I can't say that I am saved." Mother had said that the Lord had shown her that she was saved, and I felt sure that as God is no respecter of persons, he must show me that I was saved too. I could not be satisfied short of that; so I said, "Lord, I take thee as my counsellor in perplexity." Then I repeated, "Lord, I believe; help thou my unbelief." Before the sentence had dropped from my lips, I said, "Lord, I know; Lord, I know."

I can not tell you how happy I was. I arose from my knees, started out of my chamber and to my surprise met the brother with whom I had quarreled. "O Oliver," I said, "the Lord has had mercy on me and saved me." I shall never forget that day. It was May 3, 1871.

Up to that time I had not opened my heart to my father concerning my soul's condition and needs, as he was not living a satisfactory life himself, but when I went to the supper table, I was so happy that I said, "O Father, help me praise the Lord." Not knowing how my soul had been longing for God and a new life, he said, "Mary, what has broken loose?" I answered, "I can't praise Him enough; I want you to help me praise him." I was too happy to eat supper, and so went out into the yard and walked up and down praising the Lord to my soul's content.

I might say here, it was not fear of everlasting punishment that caused me to seek God, but a good faithful mother's love. I did not want to grieve her heart and as I could not keep from doing so without help from above, I sought salvation with this end in view. At this time there came very forcibly to me the scripture about Mary's anointing the Lord before his burial. I decided that she should be my example. I would give Mother some of the flowers of my experience, and not wait until after she was dead and buried. Had I waited to strew flowers over her grave, I would have expected to hear people say, "She is nothing but a hypocrite. She did not treat her mother right while she was living, and now she is trying to make a show." Let us take a lesson from Mary of old - give flowers to the living; but if we have no flowers, let us see to it that we do not give thorns. It was thorns that the enemies of Christ placed upon his brow in mockery.

Later I found that there was something in me that did not want to treat Mother just right - a disposition arising in my heart to disobey her. I felt that this grieved the Lord; and I went and asked him to forgive me. One day I said, "Mother, I am going to set down on paper a record of every day that I keep from getting mad." As I had a very high temper, Mother thought it very foolish for me to undertake such a record. Nevertheless, day after day went by in which I did not become angry, until a month had elapsed; I had not been angry for a month.

Just a month after I was saved, my oldest brother, who was a minister, came with a message on the subject of sanctification. He explained the doctrine to Mother and me and showed us our privilege of attaining to this grace. Before noon of that day we made a complete consecration for time and for eternity, grasped the promises, and both of us received the experience. I am sure that my consecration was made in great ignorance; but the Lord understood that I was sincere, and graciously granted me the experience. When I received the sanctifying grace, I did not think of demonstration, or of great feeling, or of anything of that kind: I simply consecrated all a living sacrifice, and reckoned myself dead indeed unto sin and alive unto God through our Lord Jesus Christ. I met the conditions and believed that the work was done.

Not until the tempter came, did I fully realize what God had done in sanctifying me. That evening the devil tested me in such a way that had there been any of the old Adam in me, it would have been stirred up; but, thank God! the devil found nothing to work upon. God had removed that depraved nature, the sin-principle inherited from the fall of Adam. As there was nothing but God's glory in my soul, nothing but glory could bubble up, no matter how severe the temptation. I felt so secure - just as if I were out in mid-ocean upon a solid rock, the waves dashing all around me, but powerless to disturb my security and the peace of my soul.

Soon after I was sanctified, I testified to my experience, in a Methodist quarterly meeting. The presiding elder made fun of me: he said, "The testimonies of those that claim to be sanctified, sound just like the tones of an old cracked cow-bell. There was only one good testimony made this evening; and that was by one who did not profess sanctification." My only persecution at home came from a neighbor who made fun of my prayers. Her oft-repeated expression was, "Pray like old Mary Cole." Later when her grandchild lay dying, she called on me to pray four times within twenty-four hours. After the child was dead, she said she was hurt because I did not pray for the child's healing, because she was sure that if I had done so the child would have lived.

A minister who came onto our circuit some time after this decided that those who had the experience of sanctification should not testify to it. He gave as his reason that he wanted to bring the people to a level in their experiences; in other words, he wanted to bring the sanctified ones down to lift the justified ones up, until they would all be on an equality in experience. Two sisters who were sanctified, came to me and said, "Sister Cole, we have come to the conclusion that we won't testify to sanctification this year, lest we offend the minister." I replied, "If the minister is going to oppose sanctification, so much the more will I testify to it throughout the year." I did so, and God wonderfully blessed me. These women stopped testifying to please the preacher; and before the year was out, they and the preacher were having trouble.

After I was sanctified, I was so happy and victorious in my soul, that I wanted to tell my experience to others. At one time I was talking to a lady old enough to be my grandmother, telling her how happy I was, and how I enjoyed the fulness of God's blessing. She seemed to appreciate my story greatly; but after I got through, the thought came to me that she would think that I felt myself important in trying to instruct one so much older than myself.

Although I did not know it at the time, this was the enemy whispering to me. I apologized to her for saying anything about my experience: "You must not get hurt at me because I have talked so to you, but I am very happy in the Lord." Looking at me steadily she said, "You are not worth getting hurt over." I saw the point. This was God's reproof. I learned my lesson; and so far as I know, I have never made an apology for what the Lord has done for me.

Chapter VI

Events of Early Christian Life

One day soon after I was saved, I felt God stirring within me, and gave vent to my happy soul by praising his precious name aloud. This seemed to disturb Father, and he commanded me to be quiet. But God stirred me up more and more, until my soul seemed to roar like a lion, and I quoted the following scripture to Father: "If these should hold their peace, the stones would immediately cry out." This looked like disobedience to my father; but the outcome seemed to show that God was leading me, for Father calmed down and did not again interfere with my praising the Lord.

Not long after I was sanctified, I received my first light on the subject of dress. One Sunday morning while at the Methodist meeting listening to a sermon, a voice began to talk to my soul: "You profess to be sanctified, living a holy life, and yet your head-dress shows conformity to the world." These words did not come from the pulpit either: nothing was being preached against dress or worldly conformity. Sunday after Sunday the same still, small voice talked to me in this way, until I hardly knew what to do.

Finally I said to myself, "I shall not allow my

conscience to be tortured in this way any more." Early Monday morning, therefore, as soon as I had an opportunity, I took the flowers off my hat, as they were what the Holy Spirit had been pointing out to me. My Mother, who was sitting by, said, "Mary, what are you doing?" I said, "I am taking these flowers off." "What are you doing that for?" she inquired. "Because," I answered, "I do not want them on." I did not explain matters to her just then. She replied, "That is just a foolish notion of yours. You will soon want the flowers on again." "No, Mother," I answered, "I never will."

So I took the flowers off and put them into the vase where we kept our winter bouquet. As I did so, the voice of God said, "If you do not want to be tempted in this matter again, put those flowers into the fire." I immediately obeyed, and from that day to this I have never been tempted to restore the flowers to my hat.

About ten years later while I was holding my first meeting at Salisbury, Missouri, I saw a number of young ladies who were dressed so saintlike, and in a manner so becoming to holy lives, that I was convicted immediately for plainness of dress. Some of the sisters who were gospel teachers, came to me at the close of the service, saying that they would like to have a talk with me. I thought I knew what they wanted to say, because God had already been talking to me on the same subject. I was not mistaken. "As you profess to be a holiness teacher," said they, "you ought to be an example in plainness of dress." I told them that I had no plain dresses. All I had were virtually a display of ruffles, flounces, "pin-backs" and "tuck-ups." They then inquired if I would be pleased to have them help me make my clothes over. I told them, "Certainly I would, but some of my dresses are so cut up that they couldn't be made over." I was very thankful when an opportunity was offered to make my clothes plain. God had already given me an understanding of his will in regard to dress; and it was not only easy for me to obey, but a pleasure also.

It was not so very long after this - while I was in my second meeting at Sturgeon, Mo. - that a minister handed me some money for my personal use. Soon afterwards his wife came and said that the Lord had shown her that she must give me something too. As this was the first money that had been handed me, I hardly knew what to do; but I accepted it. Then the sister said, "Now, Sister Cole, I will take the money my husband has given you and what I have given, and will buy the goods for a plain dress for you. I will see that it is made plain and neat, and so that it will fit you." How glad I was when I got that dress! Only once after that was I tempted to build again what I had destroyed. Then I got a dress and trimmed it with lace, but I could not wear it that way at all. That was my last temptation to try to dress in style.

About nine o'clock one evening in the month of December, of the year I was saved, Mother and I were in the kitchen. I was down on my knees mixing some sausage-meat in a vessel, when all at once I looked up and saw a very bright light, which seemed to be moving very rapidly. "Mother," said I, "what makes that light?" My first thought was that some of my younger brothers were carrying a light and trying to scare us; but when I saw that the light was so strong and moving so fast, I felt sure that I was mistaken. By this time mother was standing in the door and calling, "Mary, come quick and you can see what is causing the light." What I saw, was a large ball of fire. Starting from the west, or a little north of west, it moved southeast at a high rate of speed.

When we first saw the ball, about two-thirds of it was hidden behind the horizon, and we gazed at it until it went out of sight. Perhaps our imaginations worked upon our senses; but it seemed that sparks of fire flew back from the ball. In two or three minutes after the ball disappeared, there was a terrible trembling of the earth as if there had been a small earthquake. Probably the ball struck with such force that it shook the earth. This sight was witnessed by people in different states.

My feelings at the time of this incident made me think how poor sinners will feel in the day of judgment when they will be standing awaiting their doom, knowing that the wrath of God rests upon them, and that they are without hope. Far more terrifying things than the passing of a comet will be happening then; and many will be crying for the rocks and mountains to fall on them to hide them from the presence of him that liveth and reigneth forever. I confess, that though I was saved, I trembled at seeing that ball of fire in its weird passage. I thought that if this little incident had such an effect upon one who was saved and ready to meet God, what a far more terrible spectacle would the day of judgment be to those who were not ready.

One fall, not long after I was saved, the grasshoppers came to our part of the country, and laid their eggs, and in the spring the young grasshoppers hatched out by the million. There were so many grasshoppers and they destroyed the vegetation so rapidly that people began to fear a famine. The governor of the State proclaimed a day of fasting and prayer, and many people gathered at the different houses of worship to plead with the Lord to stay the plague. Even hardhearted sinners left their work and came to these meetings. God heard our petitions, and in three days the grasshoppers were gone. Then some of the unsaved people said, "Oh, well, the grasshoppers would have gone anyway. They just stayed until their wings were grown: they would have gone without prayer." Thus they dishonored God. We had an excellent crop that year - much better than usual; but when Thanksgiving time came, many of those who were at the fast-day meeting had no time to come and thank the Lord for his mercies.

Just when the grasshoppers were at their worst, my mother was making garden. Some one said, "You would better not make garden because the grass-hoppers will eat it up." "Oh, well," she replied, "I am going to plant it anyway and trust it with the Lord. 'They that sow in hope shall be partaker of their hope.'" Mother did not fight the grasshoppers at all; she just trusted the Lord.

A number of people had great battles with the grass-hoppers. I remember a doctor's wife who came to her death because of overheating herself in her exertions to keep the grasshoppers from getting her garden. Near one side of Mother's garden there was a patch of fennel. Mother saw the grasshoppers in the garden but they did not seem to take anything but the weeds. Then they moved out into the patch of fennel, stripped it of all its leaves, and left only the stems standing. I do not think Mother ever had a better garden; some of her vegetables were especially fine. "They that trust the Lord shall not be confounded."

"Blind unbelief is sure to err,
And scan his work in vain;
God is his own interpreter,
And he will make it plain."

Mary Cole

Chapter VII

My Call to the Ministry

When I was about twenty-two years of age, I attended a camp-meeting held by a number of different denominations. One night, while at this meeting, I awoke and became conscious that God was calling me to get up and to go outside the tent to pray. As I obeyed the voice of the Lord, I became conscious of his awful presence and remembered what he said to Moses: "Put thy shoes from off thy feet, for the ground whereon thou standest is holy ground." God then called to my remembrance how he had been leading me for sometime to pray in secret for many different persons and interests, and made me to understand that he wanted me to exercise myself in that way at this time also.

After I had prayed for everything I could think of, the Lord burdened me to pray again, although it seemed that I had no other language in which to express my petition. The Lord would in a special manner send down the glory in my soul and, at every repeated petition, fill me more and more with his presence. This was done at least three times. Then he confronted me with this question, "Will you consecrate yourself to go out as a life-worker for me?" "Lord," I cried, "I thought I consecrated myself all to you when I was sanctified."

"Yes, you did, but not as a life-worker," was his answer; although, of course, this was included in the "all things" that I consecrated to the Master.

Although I realized that God was talking to me, yet I began making excuses: "Lord, I am not talented; my education is so meagre; there is no one to go with me; and, besides, I have a stammering tongue." God cut my excuses short with, "Who made man's mouth? I gave Moses Aaron as his spokesman; but I will do a better part by you, I will go with you myself." Praise the Lord! Throughout the years that I have worked for him, this promise has been fulfilled.

Again, when the devil suggested that I had no means of traveling, the Lord brought to my mind this scripture, "Yea, the Almighty shall be thy defense, and thou shalt have plenty of silver." For every excuse I made, the Lord had a scripture, until I felt as did Job, that when the Almighty speaks, "I will lay mine hand upon my mouth." So I submitted and consented to obey God.

I now suppose that I was ready to go back to bed; but the Lord began to talk to me again. He showed me that he wanted me to pray still more. As I began again to pour out my heart to him, he seemed just to pour the glory into my soul and to press it down until he saw, I suppose, that I was ready to hear his plan for me - a plan that I had not yet contemplated. When he said to me therefore, "Go preach my gospel," I was astonished beyond measure. Oh, it was all so new! I made excuses; but again he gave Scripture to offset every excuse - and all so comforting and strengthening - that I submitted to his will. I went to bed almost overwhelmed by the glory of God.

Next day I thought that as I had been blessed in learning God's will concerning me, others would be rejoiced too, to hear me relate my experience. But when I began to tell publicly how God had talked to my soul, to my surprise, it stirred up a spirit of jealousy in some and before night the devil tried to carry out his design to defeat the Lord's plan in regard to me. The devil began by starting a wicked falsehood against me and thus, almost crushing the life out of me. I did not understand the devil's cunning way and did not know how to lean on God, it was a dark hour for me. I remembered how the enemies of Moses tried to slay him when he was a child, and how the Jews tried to destroy our Savior when he was a little babe. God proved himself and protected me; he lifted me above all my persecutions and made me more than a conqueror. I had learned the useful lesson to let the Lord be my defense and not to try to defend myself.

On my return home, when I told my class-leader how God had revealed his will to me concerning my future, he said, "You are a pretty looking thing to be called to preach." I thought so too; but to excuse myself, for I hardly knew what to say, I replied, "I do not believe that every one called to preach will have to stand in the pulpit: a person may preach by his life and conduct." Mother was the only other person to whom I told the story of my call, until I began my ministry.

Chapter VIII

Seven Years of Preparation

Although God had given me a very clear, definite call to the ministry, and had made very plain his purpose in regard to me, yet he did not immediately send me out to preach the gospel. Nearly seven years elapsed between the call and the sending - years in which the Lord led me and in which occurred a number of incidents that had a very important influence on my life. These together with some other incidents connected with them, which occurred in after years, will be related in this chapter.

About the time of my call to the ministry, but whether shortly before or soon afterwards, I do not remember, I was again confined to my bed from September to March. During a part of this time I was entirely helpless; but oh, with how much greater fortitude did I bear my sickness now than I did in my fifteenth year! God in his infinite love and mercy had brought about a wonderful change. Instead of being tortured and tormented, and in desperation wishing myself dead, the nearer I approached death, the happier I became. At times it seemed that the angels were hovering over me. One night I dreamed that my time had come and that I swooned away, falling into my sister's arms. I thought I heard Sister say, "Mother, she is dying." "Sister," I asked, "do you call this death?" "Yes," was the reply. "If this is death," I answered, "I could die always; it is so sweet, so heavenly, so satisfying."

But my couch at this time was not altogether a bed of roses. I suffered greatly and was easily discouraged. I realized that I needed much help and wished that God would in some way send me consolation. The voice of God's Spirit spoke directly to my soul, "If I send you consolation in a dream, will you accept it?" I answered, "Yes, Lord, any way."

That night I dreamed that I was in Father's yard, under a shade tree. Looking around me, I saw some things that were not pleasant; but when it occurred to me to look at myself, I found that I was robed in pure white. My soul was stirred as by heavenly music. Although I had never been able to sing, yet now I felt as though I could not keep from trying. My voice rang out like the clear notes of a nightingale; and all at once I was joined by a myriad of heavenly voices. The air was full of music. Peal after peal of the heavenly anthem struck upon my ear, and in my dream I exclaimed, "Is heaven so near the earth as this? Surely I hear the angels singing! Such music I have never heard upon earth!" Then I awoke with this scripture sounding in my ears: "The angel of the Lord encampeth round about them that fear him and delivereth them." Without a doubt, the angels were around me. The strength and comfort I received in my soul that night were like Elijah's meal, in the strength of which he went forty days. Even now, the thought of my experience sends a thrill of heavenly encouragement to my soul.

One evening when I was about twenty-three years old, we were having family worship, and all the saved members of the family had prayed; I felt impressed that if we should have a second season of prayer, God would do something unusual for us. As the different members of the family were praying the second time, my youngest Brother, George, ten years old, was being deeply wrought upon by the Spirit of God. He arose from his knees and started to my chair. As he was in his stocking feet, and moved noiselessly across the floor, nobody saw him. Before he got to my chair his heart failed him, and he went back to where he had been kneeling. Again the Spirit of God worked upon his heart stronger than before; he came to where I was kneeling and said, "Mary, I want to be saved too." We immediately called upon God in his behalf; the Lord wonderfully saved him; and after that he took part in family worship.

God had now given me such a love for my younger brothers that when they got into their little troubles they would come to me for help and consolation, as Mother with her large family and many cares had but little time to devote to their spiritual welfare. This small burden that God placed on me was doubtless for my good. When the boys got into little quarrels, they would come to me, and I would say to them, "Do you know the scripture, 'Only by pride cometh contention'?" "Yes." "Do you know what the matter is then?" "Yes, I am up a little." "Do you know what you have to do?" "Yes, to get down." And soon their difficulty would be settled. God wonderfully blessed my soul in thus helping my younger brothers; and all unaware to myself, I was being prepared for my future work.

I believe that I, as much as most children, always honored my father; and, after I was saved, I believe I honored him as much as God required. In the incidents I am now about to relate, I mean to cast no reflection upon the memory of my father, now many years gone to his final reward; but I tell them that they may prove a blessing to others.

My father was not living a Christian life satisfactory even to himself; and, as a result, the enemy could at times use him as his instrument. Nervous and afflicted as I was in my childhood days, I was afraid of Father when he yielded to the enemy; but after I was saved the Lord gave me much help on this line. At times however, when Father was much under the influence of the enemy, the trials were so severe that Mother and I frequently had to seek God for help two or three times a day. The Lord always came to our rescue and lifted us above the trial. When Father showed his better self, he was very dear to all of us.

When my brother Harley was about fourteen years of age, he was saved and living as true a Christian life as one would expect of a boy his age. It seemed at this time that the enemy was especially operating through Father to crush and discourage the child. God stirred up my soul to protect him and to keep him from giving way entirely. One day Harley went on an errand for Father and the mule that he rode accidentally got his ankle hurt. When he returned, Father was very much displeased, and said to my brother, "If you can do no better than that, you had better go to bed."

This was in the evening. I picked up the family Bible, walked across the room to my father and said, "We are all willing to go to bed, but we usually have family worship first. Won't you read and pray?" "You can read and pray yourself if you want to," said he. So I sat down and read, and then we knelt down and prayed; God's power came like a mighty wave from the glory world, filling the room. When we arose from our knees Father had disappeared.

A few minutes later, when one of my brothers went to the barn, Father said to him, "What is that noise at the house?" My brother answered, "God has given us the victory, and Mary is shouting." "Well," said Father, "that won't do the mule any good;" but the boy answered quickly, "Well, we weren't praying for the mule," and Father never said anything more about the injury to the mule.

At another time Harley was lying very sick, and the enemy stirred Father up to treat him cruelly. He told my brother that if he didn't get up, he would give him a good whipping. He started to get the whip. In the meanwhile, my soul was stirred to its limit; God seemed to move my very being to protect the child. I knew that he was really sick and that the enemy was using Father for his own purpose.

I went into the room where my brother was lying and stood near him. When father returned, he could see me standing by the head of the old-fashioned bedstead near one of its high posts. He knew by my looks that I was there to shield the sick boy. He ordered me out, but I made no reply. He tried to remove me by force from where I was standing; but I held on to the bedpost until finally by a strong jerk he succeeded in loosing my hold and gave me a push that threw me across the floor a number of feet away, where I fell and went to praying. God answered prayer, and gave us the victory, and Father left the room without another word. Before beginning to resist Father, I had made up my mind to take the whipping myself, rather than see my sick brother imposed upon; but God intervened, and I did not have to suffer. Every time I interfered, Father seemed to realize that it was not I, but God who was reproving him.

I was now about twenty-four or twenty-five years of age and I felt that the Lord wanted me to make a few suggestions to Father about his treatment of me. I told him that he should be careful lest he lay himself liable to the law. He answered me harshly, but it seemed that God put his fear on him, for that was the last time Father became violent toward me.

Shortly before my healing, which will be described in the next chapter, I had a very peculiar dream in which I saw the whole family sitting at the table eating. Father held in his hand an iron mallet which he began to motion in a threatening way toward Mother. I thought that he intended to take her life with the mallet. Then I thought, "Mother has been so good and kind to me that I can not bear to stay in the room and see this deed done." I started for the door. As I went, God spoke to me, saying, "Pray; ask for the strength of a Samson, if need be; and I will give it." I began praying and God answered. His strength and power came over me. I can not express how strong I felt as I went to my father, took the iron mallet out of his hand. He was like a little child in my hands. I held him until he promised he would never do so again; and all the while his face was twitching with fear, and he was trembling like a leaf.

When I was healed, God put much of his divine power into both my soul and body. It seemed that I was just filled with God and that I thrilled with his presence, until at times I was not on earth, but rather in heaven.

At one such time Father began to bring false accusations against Harley. His unkind manner, as well as the false charges, showed that he was actuated by a wrong spirit. God seemed to again stir my soul to speak in behalf of the boy. At first Father did not comprehend that God was talking through me, and spoke roughly; but he soon realized that God was using my lips of clay; the fear of the Lord came upon him, and he trembled like a leaf. I saw that God had fulfilled my dream, that he had helped me to take the iron mallet out of Father's hand. So far as I know, Father never acted so cruelly toward my brother again.

I wish to warn children who read this narrative not to use this incident to their own shame. If the Spirit of the Lord should ever lead you to resist your father or mother, he will give you the power to win a victory for truth and righteousness; but, if, on the other hand, you resist your parents in your own strength, or for selfish purposes, you will bring upon yourself shame and confusion. Even if you should succeed in having your own way, either through force of will or through your parents' meekly yielding to you, God will make you feel the shame of your wrong-doing.

In my personal dealings with Father, God manifested himself and showed himself mighty in caring for me. Once as we were going to meeting, the team became frightened and hard to hold and I became so frightened that I had a spasm after we got to meeting. Father was ashamed because I had had a spasm in public. He seemed to think he was disgraced, and concluded that in the future I should stay at home. I was now saved and sanctified and enjoyed very much attending public services, so Mother and I prayed earnestly that God would put it into Father's heart to let me attend meetings again. Our prayers were answered and I had no more difficulty until sometime afterwards. At that time I had been to a meeting several miles from home and had remained over night with some friends without asking permission. As a punishment, Father again refused to allow me to go to church.

Again Mother and I sought the Lord with prayer and fasting, and the Lord soon showed me that we had gained the victory. We felt impressed, however, to spend another day in fasting and prayer. Although Father did not know that we were praying, he came to me and said, "Mary, you can go to meeting"; and from that time he never kept me at home from services.

Father owned the farm on which we lived in Pettis County, Missouri. It contained 244 acres of fairly good land and was sufficiently stocked. Although, in a financial way, father was doing as well as his neighbors, he had for a number of years been growing discontented. These periods of discontentment seemed especially to trouble him in the spring before farm work began. At such times he wanted to mortgage his farmland and to move out of the country.

Every spring for a number of years, Mother and I would get on our knees and pray earnestly to God that he would overrule Father's roving disposition and make him content to stay at home. Again and again the dear Lord was gracious and answered our petition. Things would go on well for a while, but with the coming of the next spring, we would again have the same experience.

One spring when we took to our knees as usual to pray in behalf of Father, the Lord gave me to understand that our petition would not be answered, that Father would have his own way. This seemed almost unbearable, and I cried and prayed for Father until I almost lost my voice. God answered my petition with this suggestion: "If nothing else but to go among strangers and have a hard time will bring your father to the Lord are you willing that he should go?" I answered, "Lord, from this standpoint, but from no other." From that time the burden left me. Father went, and the Lord said to me, "Now you have no excuse for not going into gospel work." Father had been unwilling for me to go, and with his going my last excuse was removed.

Father went first to Oregon, but some years later came back as far as Wymore, Nebraska, where he bought property and settled. A few years later he came and stayed with us at home for one winter.

In a meeting that my brother George, Sister Lodema Kaser, and I held in Wymore, Father sought the Lord and seemed to get a real experience of salvation.

Later he had some little difficulty in retaining his experience. He got tried at some of the brethren and thought he would leave the church, as he had formerly done in sectarianism. He found, however, that in leaving the church he was leaving God, since people can get out of the church of God only through sin. Soon after this he began to be troubled with heart failure. He lived only a few months. My sister who cared for him in his last illness, informed me that at the time of his death he was fully restored to the fellowship of the church and that for some months before he died, he showed every sign of being prepared. God assured me that Father was saved, yet as by fire. This seemed a real miracle as much of the time Father's religious experience had not been satisfactory. We serve a mighty God who works miracles: some of Father's children had been praying so earnestly for him that God would not let them be disappointed. I believe I shall meet him in the glory world.

At the time my youngest brothers were saved, and shortly afterwards I was an invalid and unable to go to meeting on Sunday. They took turn about staying with me, while my parents went to meeting. As soon as the rest of the family were gone, we would take down the family Bible and ask the Lord to help us to turn to some scripture that would be good for us. Then we would read. Whenever we came to a promise, we would ask the Lord to help us claim that promise and to get out of it all the benefit that God had in it for us. After reading, we would get down and pray asking God to help us retain what we had read and to make it a blessing to us.

When the family would come home from meeting, Mother would tell us all she could remember of the sermon, as she was anxious to get to me all the encouragement she could. As we listened to Mother's account of the services, we realized that we had had the best meeting.

This fact became so noticeable that whenever they wanted George to go to meeting, he would say, "No, I want to stay with Mary." After the others were gone, he would say, "Mary, let us read as we did the other Sunday." "George," I would answer, "I feel so weak this morning; I don't feel able to hold the Bible" (it was a very large book), "Mary, I will hold the Bible, if you will do the reading." Weak as I was, I could not refuse, and we would begin, asking God to direct us, stopping to claim each promise, and asking God to bless the Word to our good, and to help us to remember all that would be helpful to us. We continued this practise until I was healed and able to attend the meetings again. I shall never be able to tell the profit that I derived from this little Bible school.

God himself was our teacher, and through this responsibility he was preparing me for greater usefulness.

It was during this period of apparent inactivity that God gave me my first experience of divine healing. At that time I think I was about twenty-five years of age. I was ignorant that the Lord is as willing and as able to heal our bodies as he is to save our souls. I was suffering greatly with a swelling on the inside of my jaw that entirely closed my mouth. The doctor said he would not dare to lance the swelling as the tendons and arteries lay so near that such an operation would be dangerous. He prescribed a poultice, and said that the swelling would probably break in about three days.

I went home suffering greatly: I felt that I could not endure any more. I told my two youngest brothers, who knew how to pray and cast their burdens on the Lord, to call on God earnestly that he would either relieve me of the suffering or give me grace to bear it. Soon they came to my room: one said, "I prayed for the Lord either to relieve you or give you grace to bear the pain," and the other said, "I prayed the Lord to relieve you." In ten minutes every bit of suffering was gone. A sweet calm settled over my body; and to my happy surprise, I found that the swelling had broken. It was soon gone. I suffered no more pain, and next day was able to go to meeting.

About a year later I made the acquaintance of a young man to whom I soon became greatly attached. After a time we became engaged. As I had learned to seek the mind of the Lord in all things, I did not find it hard to submit the question of matrimony to his will. The fact that I had had my own way so long, made me feel sure that the Lord was going to let me have my own way about my marriage. But this consideration did not at all affect my consecration, either at this time or when I sought God for healing. When I sought God for healing, he showed me that he wanted my entire service, and that I must seek his benefits for his glory only. It was wholly for God's glory, therefore, that I sought healing.

Perhaps some of the young ministers and workers who read this book will wonder at the long period of inactivity, as some might call it, between my call to the ministry and the time when I actually began gospel work. I now look back upon this period as a time filled with blessed experiences that moulded my character, established my faith and peculiarly fitted me for the work to which God had called me. I have always been glad that the Lord had his way. This time was not lost. Like Joseph in prison, whom God was educating to be a prince, I was being prepared in God's own way for future usefulness.

During this time of which I am now speaking, God laid it upon my heart to read the many good books, which now fell into my hands, such as Phoebe Palmer's Works - "Faith and Its Effects," "Sanctification Practical," and "Tell Jesus." The last named book was especially helpful in forming my Christian character, containing as it does so many precious experiences of trusting in God. I had the privilege also of reading the works of Mrs. Fletcher, Hester Ann Rodgers, and John Wesley. For the privilege of reading all these, I give God thanks. I put the experiences of which I read to a practical test, thus proving that what God had done for others, he would do for me also. After the test these narrations of God's marvelous dealings were no longer stories in a book, but they had become my own personal experiences.

At different times I have hunted awhile for some lost article, when the Lord would come with these words: "Tell Jesus." I would tell him and soon I would find the missing article. He would even direct me to the very spot where it lay concealed. Soon after I read the book, "Tell Jesus," I took my sewing machine apart thinking that I could clean it and put it together again, just as one of my lady friends had done. I soon found that I was not skilful enough, told Jesus, and obtained help to get the machine together all right.

Sometimes when I was not near a jeweler, my watch would get out of repair, and I would earnestly ask the Lord to fix it for me, provided he could do so without my becoming fanatical or being led wrong. A number of times he answered my prayer.

One time I remember, I let my watch fall and it was greatly damaged; but I could not get to a jeweler to have it repaired. As I felt the need of the watch very much, I asked the Lord earnestly to please fix it for me. The watch soon began running. I intended to take the watch to a jeweler later; but as it kept perfect time I did not need to take it.

During all these years God was teaching me as rapidly as he could, lessons of faith and trust. In every severe trial or test, no matter what its nature, I would earnestly lay my trouble before God and he would marvelously lift me up and give me victory. At such times he would give me precious promises such as these: "When the enemy comes in like a flood, the Spirit of the Lord shall lift up a standard against him;" "The desire of the righteous shall be granted;" "They that trust in the Lord shall not be confounded, and shall not lack any good thing."

From the beginning, my spiritual life was one of trials; but thank God, the trials were always followed by triumphs. "Thanks be to God who giveth us the victory through our Lord Jesus Christ." In such experiences, I learned what has been verified to me again and again throughout the course of my life, that it pays to cast all our cares and burdens upon him who has promised to bear them for us; to leave everything with him; to lay ourselves and all we possess at his feet, tiusting him to care for us and to carry our sorrows. God wants just such an opportunity. He is a wonderful God, a very present help at all times. "They that trust in the Lord shall be as Mount Zion, which can not be moved, but abideth forever." "As the mountains are round about Jerusalem, so is the Lord round about his people from henceforth even forever."

Dear young ministers and workers, God may call you to his work and send you forth at once into the field; but do not be impatient or discouraged if the Lord sees fit to have you tarry awhile after he has called you. Remember, you are implements in the hands of the Lord. As workers called of the Lord, you should be like clay for the Master's use. Be careful, however, lest you become marred in God's hands as was the vessel that Jeremiah saw in the hands of the potter.

Do not get in God's way and so spoil his design. Remember that Jesus at twelve years old knew that he must be about his Father's business; but he was thirty before he began his ministry. Remember that John the Baptist tarried in the wilderness for a long time before he began preaching on the banks of Jordan. Remember that the disciples spent ten days in the upper room before power came upon them from on high. You know this; nor do you think that these times of tarrying were wasted. Neither will your time of waiting be lost. Abide God's time; then, when you do enter upon your ministry, you will go, sustained by his power and by his blessing.

Chapter IX

Healed by Divine Power

I have now to relate what to me is one of the most important events of my life. Up to this time I had been a hopeless invalid. The doctors could not cure me. Under the care of some, my health would improve for a short time; but others would not undertake to do anything for me. After inquiring into my condition, they would say that it would be as easy to make a world as to restore me to health. I remember especially that this remark was made by the doctor who was attending me shortly before my healing. At the time I was healed, my case was in the hands of a specialist, who said he could give me no permanent relief in less than a year.

Having no hope of help from the doctor and having been taught that the days of divine healing were past, I concluded that there was no hope for me, and that the Lord intended me to be made perfect through suffering. In the spring of 1880, my oldest brother, who had been greatly afflicted with chronic dyspepsia, was healed in answer to prayer. Not until that time did I know that any one had been healed by divine power since the days of the apostles. I did not consider the healing which I have already related a healing, but a special miracle performed in answer to prayer. As he and I were the invalids of the family, we naturally sympathized a great deal with each other, opened our hearts to each other, shared all our troubles and sorrows.

During the summer of the year I have just mentioned, my brother came home and began to tell how well he was. "Jeremiah, what patent medicine have you been taking?" He looked at me, smiled and said, "Mary, if you will take the kind of medicine I have, you will be well too." "What kind is that?" "It is faith and prayer - the Lord's word received by faith." This was all new to me - just like a strange language. I asked no more questions, for I did not know what to say.

Finally, Mother, who had been listening to the conversation, said to him, "Can you eat a raw egg if I get it for you?" His health had been so poor that at times he could eat nothing but a raw egg, and frequently he would refuse even that. "Mother," he replied, "I can eat two eggs if you can spare that many, and you may cook them for me." When Mother cooked the eggs, he looked at her and said, "Mother, have you any meat?" She looked at him doubtfully, and not comprehending what God had done for his body, said, "I don't believe I will give you any meat this time." He made no reply, knowing that she did not understand.

It was October before I saw my brother again. Another swelling had appeared on my jaw, stopping my mouth so that I could take my food only in a liquid form, sucking it through my teeth. My brother again encouraged me to trust the Lord, quoting God's promises to heal the body and relating a number of instances that he had witnessed where persons were healed of fits and other serious afflictions. I told my brother that I did not doubt that the Lord had healed others, but said that I did not know whether or not he wanted to heal me. "Perhaps," said I, "he is leaving me afflicted to keep me humble. If I were healed, I might not keep saved." My brother showed me that God was just as willing to heal me as he was to heal anybody else, and that it was both my duty and privilege to trust God for my healing. "Look over your consecration," said he "and see if you are willing to be healed for God's glory alone."

I thought the matter over for some days. One day I prayed for my healing until I thought I could claim it by faith; but I soon found that the work was not done. Upon waking a few mornings later, I said to myself, "I am going to let the Lord heal me today if he will." Then the enemy whispered, "You have not enough faith yet to be healed; put it off a week or two, and by that time your faith will be stronger." Then came the voice of Jesus, "Oh thou of little faith; wherefore didst thou doubt." Dropping on my knees, I cried "Lord if it is unbelief, take it out root and branch"; and I knew he did. Then I said, "Lord, what next?" He then showed me I should pour out my medicine. God revealed to me that I was to be severely tempted, and that if I had any medicine about, that I would be sure to take it and so lose faith for healing.

God was now bringing me to a place where I must choose between trusting God and disbelieving his promises. As a first act of faith on my part, I poured out my medicine. God showed me that if I were to doubt the Scriptures: "Who healeth all thy diseases"; "The prayer of faith shall save the sick," etc, I would not stop until I should reject all his Word, die an infidel, be lost in hell, and perhaps be the means of the loss of scores of other souls.

I said to Mother, "If you ever prayed earnestly for me, pray now." So we bowed together. After she prayed, I began praying, claimed the promise in Matthew 18:19: "Lord, thou hast said, that if two shall agree on earth as touching anything that they shall ask, it shall be done for them of the Father which is in heaven. Now, Lord, we are agreed that thou shalt heal me - soul, mind, body, and spirit as completely as is most to thy glory." As I said this, I laid hold on the healing power by faith, the witness came from heaven, and the work was done. I arose from my knees saying, "Mother, it is done! I am healed! I am healed!" I felt the virtue go through my body; and, oh, the showers of heavenly grace that filled my soul! I began to praise the Lord. Oh, it was heavenly! "My soul was joyful in glory," for God filled my soul. Then was fulfilled that which was spoken by the prophet Isaiah saying, "Then shall the lame man leap as an hart and the tongue of the dumb sing: for in the wilderness shall waters break out and streams in the desert" (Isaiah 35:6).

This was the beginning of a new epoch in my life, the beginning of months to me. It was the first time in my recollection that I could say I was well: the first bright hope of health that I had ever had in this world. That same day I could eat and drink without the slightest distress, anything that was fit for a sound stomach. I had never been able to do this before.

But that night the trial came. It seemed that all hell was let loose to try to rob me of my healing faith and to bring back all my diseases. Had I not poured out my medicine, I surely would have yielded. Having no other refuge, I clung to the promises of God, and rebuked the devil until 2 o'clock in the morning. Then I saw fulfilled God's promise: "Resist the devil and he will flee from you"; and there was a great calm. It seemed that the angels came and ministered unto me. My joy was full; my cup ran over. When morning came I began praising the Lord; and for several days, I walked the floor offering almost ceaseless praises to God. The story was circulated throughout the neighborhood, "Mary Cole is having a whole camp-meeting by herself. She claims that God has healed her; but as soon as the excitement wears off, she will be as bad as ever."

My appetite was now good, and my strength increased daily. Soon I was able to attend a protracted meeting held by the Methodists, of which denomination I was still a member. When opportunity was given for testimonies, I arose and told of God's wonderful dealings with me - how he had pardoned all my sins, made me his child, afterwards sanctified me wholly, and how he had recently healed my poor afflicted body. I exhorted them to get rid of unbelief and to move out for God on the Bible promises. After meeting, the preacher came to talk to me about my experience. He said he did not doubt that I had been healed, but I must not testify to it, "for" said he, "the people can not stand so much light."

I very foolishly concluded to follow the preacher's advice; and immediately the flood-gates of hell seemed to open. The powers of darkness seemed to gather to destroy both soul and body - my mind was almost reeling; intense suffering began in my body. God showed me that I had broken my contract with him in order to please a blinded preacher. My feelings were indescribable. I did not know what to do; but God showed me that if I would renew my covenant with him, resist the devil, and obey God in all things, all would be well. I obeyed God, and my faith again became unwavering; my strength began to increase; and a large scrofulous ulcer that had appeared on my face, soon went away. My blood became pure; and warmth, such as I had never felt before, came into my body. I could now sleep comfortably with half as much covering on my bed as I formerly required.

Since my first healing, I have had a few attacks of sickness but God has healed me every time. In the thirty-four years that have elapsed since I began to trust the Lord for the healing of my body, I have never resorted to doctors, nor have I taken any medicine. I have been as well as the average person, and have been able to do work as hard as God has required of me. I recommend God as a physician. At the time I was healed of my other bodily afflictions, I was also relieved of stammering. It is true I stammer some yet, at times, but not nearly so much as I did formerly; and not enough to prevent my preaching the Word.

At the time of my healing, Marion, one of my unsaved brothers, was batching near the old home place. He frequently spent his evenings at home, sometimes lying on chairs drawn up in front of the old-fashioned fireplace. On the Wednesday after I was healed, I found him lying before the fire and said to him, "Oh, Marion, have you heard the good news? The Lord has healed me." And he said, "Do you mean that he has healed you or that he has healed that sore on your face?" "I mean that he has healed me, sore and all." Then I went out of the room praising the Lord. Near the close of that same week, Marion attended the revival meeting then going on at the M. E. Church, came to the altar, and got gloriously saved. Mother went to speak to him and to rejoice with him. "The Lord has been good to you, my son, to save you." "Yes," he answered, "I thought if the Lord could heal Mary when the doctors gave her up, he could save a poor sinner like me."

In the years that have passed since the Lord so graciously healed me, I have witnessed many cases of healing. One that especially appealed to me occurred in December, 1880, at the Jacksonville, Illinois, Holiness Convention, where my brother Jeremiah first met D. S. Warner. I was not a witness to this incident, but I relate it as my brother, who was present, told the story.

A lady by the name of Sarah Gillillen, who was afflicted with a very bad internal cancer, came to that meeting. Several months before the doctors had told her that her case was beyond their skill. She felt impressed that she would be healed at this meeting, and Jeremiah, Brother Warner, and others were very much interested in her case. They sought to encourage her and to strengthen her faith as they had opportunity. Her faith in God seemed to increase rapidly.

One Sunday morning she said that the Lord had shown her that if she would get up that morning and testify to her healing he would finish the work. She got up before the large audience and began to give her testimony. A rule had been adopted that if any one testified too long, the congregation should sing him down. As Sister Gillillen testified for some time, they started to sing her down; but one of the ministers said, "Brethren, let her alone. This thing is of God." She continued her testimony; but before she got through, the power of God came down, her face shone with glory, and right then and there God finished her healing. She was made perfectly well.

Chapter X

Entering the Gospel Field

During the seven years that had elapsed since my call to preach the gospel, years in which God had so wonderfully taught me and so gently led me, I never doubted my call. By the help and grace of God I had been able to live pleasing to the Lord, and throughout the entire time had no knowledge of his condemnation or displeasure.

I was still engaged to the young man of whom I have already spoken; and after my healing, began to make preparations for the wedding. I was fully submitted to the Lord on the question of matrimony; but as my life had been running along in such a pleasant, even course, and as I had been having my own way in nearly everything, I felt that God was going to let me have my way in this matter also, when to my surprise, God made clear to me that I should not marry. He showed me that he had chosen me for himself, and that he had first right. He brought to my mind such scriptures as this: "Thy maker is thy husband; the Lord of Hosts is his name." As I submitted, the Lord did not leave me comfortless. He showed me that I was not able to fulfil both the mission he had given me, and the life that I had contemplated.

For so long a time now since my call to the gospel work I had been at home enjoying the companionship of my mother and of my brothers and sisters, doing the little things that God had given me to do, and feeling the approval of God upon my soul, I had failed to seek God earnestly to see if he would have me move out in active gospel work. In May of the year 1882, my brother Jeremiah, who had been out in the active ministry, returned home. One day he said to me, "Mary, did not the Lord call you to preach his gospel?" "Yes," I replied. "Has he not shown you that that is your future work?" "I thought he had in the past, but it is not clear now." "Do you want to know why it is not clear to you now?" My brother then showed me that I had not been as diligent as I should in seeking to know God's will in the matter, that I had taken too much for granted that the Lord would have me continue doing as I had been for the past seven years. He asked me to pray about going with him into the work at that time. I did as he requested; but, as I was not anxious for an answer, did not pray earnestly enough, and as a result, no answer came.

It was not long until Jeremiah asked me if I had prayed about my going with him into the work. I answered that I had, but when he asked me what the Lord had shown me, I was obliged to say, "Nothing." "Well," he replied, "As you are not decided I suppose I would better go right on to the meeting of the holiness association at Salisbury and not wait for you." Seeing that my brother was not satisfied with my answer, I again went to prayer. This time I called upon God with all my heart; and the Lord showed me that I could go into the ministry and be saved or I could stay at home and lose my soul.

Doubtless no young minister, no matter how conse-crated he may be to the will of God, finds it easy to take his first step in gospel work. I was no exception to the rule. Twice already when I arose in the public assembly to bear witness to God's dealings with me, my testimony became an exhortation, and God spoke through me to the edification of the people; but I had so far done no preaching, and now that I had reached the decision to go with my brother into the active ministry, I was conscious of conflicting emotions. On the one hand, I was glad to go in obedience to God, and on the other I hesitated to take the first step. Besides the natural human shrinking from taking the first step, I knew how Mother would feel about my going, and felt bad to grieve one who had been so kind to me. You must understand, however, that Mother's feeling about my going into gospel work was very different from Father's opposition of which I have already spoken.

At the time I broke the news to Mother, she was going through a severe trial. It was about a week after I had my talk with Jeremiah. "Mother," said I, "if you had a child that had been afflicted with a disease that had baffled the skill of all the physicians she had consulted, and finally one physician undertook the case and performed the cure with the consideration that your child should go and work for him whenever and wherever he wished; would you let the child go?" Mother said, "I know just what you mean. If nothing else will do, you may go." "Mother, as I go out into an unfriendly world, I do not expect to have an easy time; but I believe it would not be so hard to endure the buffetings of the world, if I could look back and think that my mother gave me up gladly to the Lord, who has done so much for me." We went into earnest prayer and God gave us victory over the trial. When a week later Mother accompanied me to the train, there were no tears in our eyes. Almost five years passed before I saw her face again.

Before starting from home, Mother had said to me, "Mary, here is a little change to buy your stamps and envelopes." As I reached out my hand, my brother said, "Mary do not take that money; Mother will need it. The Lord will provide you with stamps and envelopes." I thought, "Why does he talk that way? Even if he can trust God, I can't; and he ought to let me take the money." He knew better than I. The Lord provided all the stamps and envelopes I needed. Indeed, I do not remember a time that I had to wait long to write a letter for the want of stamp or envelope. As I exercised myself in trusting the Lord, my faith grew; so that I had no fear but that God would provide everything I needed - my carfare, my clothing, and even a little money to give to the cause.

The first place my brother and I visited was Salisbury, Missouri, where a holiness convention was being held. A large concourse of people from all parts of the United States were assembled in the large new tobacco factory, which at that time had not been used. When we reached the place, the meeting had been in session for several days. A number of souls had been saved; but at the time of our arrival, not many of the people felt the power of conviction.

On the Sunday after our arrival, the minister who had charge of the meeting got up and said, "The Lord has not given me a message this morning, but he has given a message to some one here. If the person who has the message does not deliver it, he will be responsible."

The pulpit was filled with ministers, and workers were sitting all around nearby. I was on my feet in a moment. I had a message from heaven - burning words that went right into the hearts of the people. God made my tongue as the pen of a ready writer. The power of God was on me in such measure that I could hardly tell whether I was in heaven or on earth. Even old men bowed themselves and wept like children, and sinners came flocking to the altar. Thank God for the blessing and encouragement that he gave me in delivering this my first public message!

As soon as the service was ended, a merchant of the town came and invited me to his home for dinner. I wondered why he should ask me to dinner; but when he began to ask me all the difficult religious questions that he could think of, the mystery was explained. I felt my inability and ignorance as I never had before, and leaned heavily on God for wisdom. The scripture, "I will give you in that hour what ye ought to say," was fulfilled.

After a number of difficult questions had been asked, my host said, "I want to ask you one more question." Supposing that this question would be so difficult that it would be impossible for me to answer, I called on God more vehemently than ever. Then came the question: "If you should die now, without a moment's warning, do you know that you are ready?" I was agreeably surprised. That was an easy question to answer. "Yes," said I, with the utmost assurance. "I wish," said his wife, "I could say that"; and a lady who was present added, "I think I would have to pray before I should be ready."

In my early evangelistic work I met considerable

opposition to woman's preaching, and at nearly every meeting I had to explain the Scriptural teaching on this subject. Nearly all opponents to woman's preaching fortified themselves with such scriptures as these: "It is a shame for a woman to speak in the church"; "Suffer not a woman to teach or to usurp authority," etc. The Lord helped me to successfully drive these opposers out of their false positions and to show them that they were misusing the Scriptures.

In this connection, too, I would call attention to 1 Corinthians 11:5, which gives instructions how a woman should pray or prophesy. If a woman be instructed how to prophesy, she surely is granted the right to prophesy. The New Testament definition of "prophesy" is: "He that prophesieth speaketh unto men to edification, exhortation and comfort." If, then, a woman be allowed to prophesy; that is, to speak unto men to edification, exhortation, and comfort, she is granted all the privileges that any minister enjoys.

We read also in Acts 1:14 that after the ascension when the disciples gathered in the upper room, "There all continued with one accord in prayer and supplication, with the women, and Mary, the mother of Jesus, and with his brethren," which scripture proves that there were women present at the Pentecostal baptism. After the descent of the Holy Spirit upon those assembled, Peter says (Acts 2:16,17), "But this is that which is spoken by the Prophet Joel; And it shall come to pass in the last days, saith God, I will pour out of my Spirit upon all flesh: and your sons and daughters shall prophesy, and your young men shall see visions and your old men shall dream dreams." We see then, according to the prophecy of Joel, that the daughters as well as the sons were to prophesy.

According to Acts 2:4, they all spake as the Spirit gave them utterance. Does not the "all" include the women present? Was not their speaking as the Spirit gave utterance the act of a minister in preaching?

In Romans 16:1 Paul says, "I commend unto you Phoebe, our sister, which is a servant of the church which is at Cenchrea." Is not the servant of the church the minister? When they used to tell me that this scripture means that a woman could serve the church only by doing temporal work, such as cooking for ministers, etc., I would answer, "If the inference of this scripture is that a woman can serve the church by doing temporal work only, the preachers are not doing their duty, because in the second verse the Lord commanded the other ministers to assist Phoebe. If then the women's only service be to cook for the ministers, the ministers, if they would obey this scripture, should certainly help the women cook."

Before going to our second meeting, at Sturgeon, Missouri, I had learned that the women in that place were not allowed to preach. On my arrival I asked some of the women if the sisters had liberty. "Yes," said they, "to pray and sing, and to testify a little." "Well," said I, "I can't sing; but I can pray, and 'testify a little.'" I learned that during this meeting a petition to license a saloon in the town had been drawn up and that a number of the women in attendance at the meeting had signed the petition. During the latter part of the meeting God's Spirit fired my soul to preach the Word, but I had no opportunity. I counseled with some of the ministers about it and received conflicting advice. Some said, "Sister Cole, you know the restrictions; you would better not preach." Others said, "Go ahead, Sister Cole: God will see you through." On the last night of the meeting, whenever I would decide to speak, God would bless my soul; but when I would decide to keep still, it seemed as if I should be paralyzed. One brother made a remark that had a strong tendency to keep me from speaking that evening: "If you get up on the last night of the meeting," said he, "it will look as if you were taking advantage of the man who has the meeting in charge." Finally, after two of the brethren had spoken for a short time, I felt clear to take the floor, and God spoke through me in power.

I reminded them of the petition to license the saloon for the purpose of damning souls, and sending them to hell, and spoke of the women's names that had been signed to the petition to license the saloon. "From childhood," said I, "I have heard that woman is the downfall of this world. She is now offered the opportunity to destroy souls, but it is a shame and a disgrace to any town that its women are not allowed to preach in the church to help save souls. Before I came to this meeting, I knew the restrictions; but I made up my mind that if I was thrown into the furnace of trial, I would go into that furnace praying for the one that had put the restrictions upon me."

The power of God wonderfully attended the message. At the close of the meeting, a wealthy gentleman, the one who had denied women the privilege of speaking, came and wanted to shake hands with me. "May the Lord bless you," said I, extending my hand. "I believe the Lord blesses you," he answered. I replied that he did. I was told later that on the next day he told certain persons on the street that doubtless that little girl was relieved since she had got her mouth off.

At the time of which I now speak, I had never heard a woman preach. My own preaching had been done by God's power and under his anointing. At about the time the Sturgeon meeting closed, I heard of a woman preacher some forty miles away, and felt quite anxious to meet her. In company with my brother, I went to visit her and found a dear saint of God who had been used much in the salvation of souls. She had taken a severe cold, which had later settled on her lungs; and at the time of our visit, her affliction had developed into consumption, and she was growing rapidly worse. It seemed that her faith could not grasp God's promises for healing.

We wanted to help the sister all we could, but I had been working very hard, washing and ironing, and was feeling quite exhausted; so much so, indeed, that I did not feel like sitting up while my brother was talking to her. As I was lying on the couch trying to rest, my brother said, "Mary, is there anything you want from the Lord?" "Nothing," said I, "unless it be rest." "Well," said he, "if you can take the Lord for it, he can rest you in an instant." The words were scarcely uttered before my faith grasped the Lord; I was rested from head to foot, jumped off the bed, and fairly bounced up and down with joy, feeling as though I had never been tired. The sister for whom we had been praying, remarked, "That gets away with my faith." "Do you doubt my having been tired?" I asked. "No." "Do you doubt the Lord's resting me?" "No; but I never saw it on this fashion."

That afternoon we took the train for Jefferson City, Missouri. After we arrived at our destination, my brother hunted a place for me to board while he went about sixty miles into the country to get a team and wagon to take us to our new field of labor, there being no railroads in that direction.

After a day or two, the lady with whom I boarded learned that I was a gospel worker. "If I can get a congregation together," said she, "will you talk to them?" I told her that I would. The people come together, and I asked some one to lead in prayer, but no one made any response. Finally they said that there was a man across the street who could pray, and asked if they should call him. The man came in; he and I led in prayer, and the Lord gave me a message. After the service was over, different ones came and congratulated me, saying, "It was a grand message; you highly entertained us," just as if I were an actress and they came for no other purpose than to be entertained. A number of those present were professors of religion; but I doubted whether there were any possessors.

For a time the woman with whom I was staying seemed quite suspicious of me, but God helped me to live so that before the week was out she had perfect confidence in me, and sometimes left her house in my care all day. I helped her what I could about her housework; and at her request, held as many as three cottage meetings during the week. God gave me favor with the woman; for when I went away she charged me only half the usual price for my board and lodging, and even gave me some presents. She did not know that I paid her all the money I had; but the Lord knew all about it, and saw to it that she did not charge me too much.

My brother had now come with a team and wagon. Accompanied by the owner of the outfit, we started on our difficult journey to our new field of labor. The roads were very rough and rocky, and we met with some hardships. We tried to camp out one night, but the mosquitos were so bad we had to resume our journey as soon as we could see to travel in the morning. Before we reached our destination, our provisions well-nigh gave out. At the end of our journey we had nothing left but a little stale bread and some bacon. Having no chance to cook anything, we made our last meal on dry bread and raw bacon.

Chapter XI

Labors in a New Field

For the next three years my brother and I worked in Missouri, in territory lying in Maries, Phelps, Pulaski and Miller counties. The country was very rough and hilly. Many of the people were very wicked - most of them being of the type that live in a rough country remote from railroads.

A Baptist minister whom we met soon after we began work in this part of the State, is a fair illustration of the religious standard of the people. This man, who, for the want of a better name, we shall call Father B - , a name by which he was known far and near, was called on all occasions where a minister was needed throughout a territory twenty or thirty miles in extent. He served as evangelist and pastor, and officiated at weddings and funerals. The people among whom he labored supported him quite liberally; but he used the money they gave him in buying whiskey, and spent a good share of his time in a drunken, or semi-drunken condition.

He used frequently to attend our meetings, because as he expressed it, he liked "to hear the woman preacher." Very frequently he staggered into meeting supported by the man who accompanied him, and sometimes had to be supported after he was seated. His seat on the front bench of the small country schoolhouse in which the meetings were held, brought him so near me that the offensive smell of his breath sickened me almost beyond endurance, and I could scarcely continue my sermon. Yet this man, habitual drunkard as he was, and filthy with tobacco, was considered throughout that region worthy of financial support and of the title and office of minister.

About fifteen years before we went to that country, a certain woman, who for many years now has been a true sister in the church, had been saved in one of Father B - 's meetings, obtaining, as she has always believed, a real experience of salvation. But when she saw that Father B - drank whiskey and chewed tobacco, she became discouraged and took to attending parties and dances. When called before the church to give an account of her conduct, she defended herself by saying that she did not think it any worse for her to attend parties and dances, than it was for the preacher to drink whiskey and to chew tobacco. I do not now remember what action the congregation took in regard to her; but at any rate, she went into sin, and lost her experience. This sister came to our meetings, sought the Lord, and was again restored to divine favor.

Father B - was a very old man when we first met him. He died before we left that part of the country. His last illness was preceded by a drunken spree, during which some rougish boys painted a barren fig-tree on his bald head. He died soon afterward. Notwithstanding the efforts of those who prepared the body for burial, his head went to its last resting-place still marked by some of the paint that portrayed him as a barren fig-tree.

But not all of the people had such a low conception of religion. God had some true children in that part of the country. My brother had already held meetings in these countries; God had blessed his efforts; and a number of souls had been saved and sanctified. Nevertheless, when we arrived, the outlook for holding meetings was not good. It was now late in the fall - too late for outdoor meetings - so we began holding services in small schoolhouses. The people came out in crowds. God's Spirit worked on their hearts, and numbers came to the Lord.

You must not suppose, however, that any one could preach the straight gospel very long in such a place without meeting opposition. One night while my brother and I were holding our first series of meetings, at a schoolhouse on Dry Creek, in Maries County, Missouri, a mob of about a dozen drunken men came with the intention of breaking up the meeting. When they came, the service had not yet begun. The men entered the room in a boisterous way, talking loudly, and acting in an offensive insulting manner toward every one in the room. I do not remember just how it came about, but for some reason one of the men caught hold of my brother and gave him a jerk that sent him whirling for some distance across the room. I was afraid that Jeremiah was in danger; but when I saw that he was not at all frightened, my fears subsided. There was so much noise and loud talking, however, that we could not begin the meeting, so we offered earnest prayer that the Lord would take charge of things and quell the disturbance. I tried to preach, but there was still too much confusion.

While I was standing in the pulpit, one of the drunk men near the door pointed a revolver at me, but God protected me: the weapon did not go off. The man who had pointed the revolver at me, soon went out, accompanied by his comrades and by a number of other men who wanted some of the whiskey. Some of the women went to the door to beg their husbands and brothers to come in, and stood there crying, fearful that their relatives would be killed. I went to the door and said to the women, "Come in. If there is any trouble you can do nothing to prevent it." "We would come in too," said one of the rowdies, "but you always begin on us." "No," I answered, "we will not begin on you. We shall be glad to have you come in, and we shall expect you to behave yourselves."

Most of the men outside came in, and the meeting began. The Lord gave me the message. During my discourse, I said, "Fools make a mock at sin, but who is it that mocks God?" "No fools, no tun. You know that too," cried one of the men. Then he began to say the Lord's prayer, but was too drunk to finish it. I paid no attention to the interruption, and continued my sermon. There was no more disturbance, and not a revolver was fired until the mob was some distance from the house. One of the men gave himself up the next day and three others were arrested. They were a shamefaced set of fellows after it was all over.

Early in December we were holding meeting on Dry Creek not far from where we held our first series of meetings in Meries county. Some grown-up boys and girls, who had been drinking freely, came to the services and created such a disturbance that Jeremiah thought it best in the interest of good order to have them arrested. On the day of the trial the two lawyers employed to defend these young men and women, ridiculed and belittled my brother, calling him "the immaculate Jeremiah," and insinuating that he thought himself almost equal to Christ. At first I felt greatly tried, but when I looked round and saw that Jeremiah's face was glowing and that he seemed almost happy enough to shout, my burden all left me. I made up my mind that since my brother was so triumphant I, too, would throw off the burden and claim victory. The young people who had disturbed the meeting had to pay a small fine. So far as I know, they behaved better in the future.

Just a few days after the occurrence just related, we began a meeting in the Bell schoolhouse, about five miles further down Dry Creek. My brother and I were staying with different families in the district. An M. E. South preacher who lived in the neighborhood, and who had heard of our trouble with the young folks in the other district, sent word to my brother that a mob was coming that night to break up our meeting, and that we should stay away and let him hold that service. He believed that the young people opposed us because we taught holiness, divine healing, etc.; and thought that his age, and the confidence of the people of the neighborhood in him would enable him to control the mob and to hold the meeting without difficulty. He tried to send word to me too; but, as I was staying with a family who lived some distance away, I did not receive his message. Jeremiah remained at his boarding place.

I went to the schoolhouse that evening expecting nothing unusual; but to my surprise I found in the house and yard a boisterous crowd of twenty-five or thirty men, who had been drinking freely of the liberal supply of whiskey they had brought with them. They were banded together for the express purpose of having a good time and breaking up the meeting. I can give you no adequate idea of the scene that greeted me as I approached. Men were running in and out of the schoolhouse, drinking, yelling, swearing, and talking at the top of their voices. The confusion was terrible.

Soon after my arrival the old preacher attempted to begin the service. He gave out a song, which a few of those present tried to sing; but the crowd was so noisy that the preacher alternately plead with them and reproved them, but without avail. The noise increased: the confusion became so great that, in despair, the old preacher gave up the attempt to hold a meeting and began to take down the names of those members of the mob whom he knew. The men had with them a number of bottles and jugs of whiskey. Drinking, swearing, and yelling continued without intermission, and from time to time we could hear the firing of revolvers. As soon as it seemed safe to do so, I went home with one of my friends, who lived near by.

As soon as possible, the old minister had a number of the members of the mob arrested and brought to trial for disturbing the peace. The preacher's actions during the trial showed that his object was, not so much to preserve the peace, as to take vengeance. Not content with a fine, he insisted on a jail sentence.

After the prosecution had offered its evidence against the mob, the lawyers on the defense made fun of the preacher saying: "What! you! A minister of the gospel! You want to send them to jail! You should be praying for them and trying to get them saved." His reply was, "Yes, I will do all I can to send them to prison and then I will go and grin at them (in derision) through the bars." I do not now recall whether or not the culprits received any punishment; but at any rate, the preacher's desire for vengeance was not satisfied. It was a common report about the country that he was so disappointed and mortified over what had happened that he did not sleep any that night. The difference of spirit manifested by my brother and that manifested by the old preacher shows the difference between the operation of the love of God and of human vengeance.

Soon after we began our labors, I became afflicted with the itch, which was then epidemic in that part of the country. A neighboring high school had been closed because of this disagreeable affliction. Previous to taking the disease myself, I had met some of the saints who had it, and who had not been healed as soon as I thought they should be. I shall have to relate that through ignorance - to my shame, be it said - I was not as compassionate to those unfortunate ones as I should have been. I had made assertions similar to this: "If you can't trust the Lord for healing, I would advise you to use remedies. Mother says that any one who would keep such an affliction any length of time is not decent." Many of the people were wounded because of my heartless way of talking, though I did it ignorantly.

The Lord saw that I needed a good lesson, and therefore let the malady come upon me in a severe form. While preaching in small overheated school-houses with but very poor ventilation, my body became overheated, thus aggravating the disease, and soon I was not able to be in the public services at all. My arms swelled so that I could not straighten them; and for some months, I had but little use of my hands. This affliction baffled my faith more than any that I had had up to that time, but I had no temptation to resort to remedies. The case of the lady preacher whom we visited in northern Missouri stood before me as a warning. I decided to have my battle now, and not to give way and lose my healing faith. So I held on steadily by the help of my brother and fought the battle through until God gave me victory.

It was some time before I got rid of all the symptoms. The Lord showed me that I must be willing to go into the work again with them still showing. To do so, required humility, and I had to seek the Lord for help. I met rebuffs of which only the Lord and I knew; but God was ordering this experience, and the trial lasted no longer than was for my good. To complete the lesson, God laid upon me the duty of confessing publicly the attitude I had held towards those who had the itch before me, and the way I had talked to them. I made my confession, humbly asking the forgiveness of all who had been wounded by my words. God's way is humility before honor. The going down is painful; but God's lifting up afterwards is sweet. Praise his dear name! Christ was a meek and lowly Savior. To follow his example we must go the lowly way.

While yet in sectarianism I got the impression that the devil had to be stirred before a good revival could be held. Acting on this principle, I prayed that the Lord would stir the devil in the series of meetings my brother and I were then beginning at the Tennyson schoolhouse.

My prayer was answered. One evening near the beginning of this revival nine respectable young men of Vichy, Missouri, hired horses and saddles at the livery barn and came out to the schoolhouse to attend the meeting. Two desperate characters, reputed to have escaped from the penitentiary, were present, but remained outside the house. The services proceeded unmolested; but, after the service, when the nine young men from Vichy went to get their horses, they found that some one had cut the saddles and bridles in pieces and turned their horses loose. Others found their harness cut and the nuts of their wagons gone. The two desperadoes now began walking back and forth through the yard, displaying their weapons and threatening to shoot any one that accused them of committing any depredation. As the burrs had been removed from the wagon in which I came, I had to ride home on a mule behind another person. Jeremiah said, "Mary, I hope you have learned the lesson to not pray the Lord to stir the devil until you know you are able to cast him out. It is not always necessary that the devil be stirred before a revival. Souls can be saved and even devils cast out without the devil's being stirred and the power of the enemy being put on exhibition." I never again prayed for the devil to be stirred.

About the beginning of the new year, the affliction which I have already mentioned, rendered me unfit for public service, and for about three months my brother and I stayed at the home of Brother Baugh on Dry Creek, where we read and studied and prayed and fought the affliction that had been imposed upon us. My brother got his prayers through and obtained healing much sooner than I. He used afterward to say, "I shall thank God through all eternity for having had the itch; because when I prayed through for healing, I struck the evening light," meaning that he was beginning to discern the unity of God's people. This remark was often followed by a happy, hearty laugh.

Early in the spring I had so far recovered from my affliction that my brother and I began again to hold meetings in the schoolhouses in the counties where we had been working, covering in all a territory about fifteen or twenty miles in extent. These meetings usually lasted two, three, and four weeks at each place, and were very profitable in the salvation of souls. There were some things in connection with our work, however, that puzzled us greatly. For instance, after we had held a good meeting in which a number of souls had been saved, and had gone on to other appointments, preachers of different denominations would follow us up, preaching against two works of grace and divine healing, and casting reflections on us as ministers, with the result that upon returning after an absence of several weeks, we would find the people discouraged, and the congregation in a bad spiritual condition.

These things made our hearts ache. We saw that in our absence the people needed some one to give them advice, encouragement, and spiritual help.

Finally my brother said to me, "Mary, I am going to write to the Free Methodists and ask them if they will send us a preacher that will preach holiness." It was not long until we received the following letter from the Free Methodist Conference: "If you get a congregation large enough to guarantee a minister a salary of five or six hundred dollars a year, we will send you a man that believes in holiness." As they did not say that the minister they would send would have the experience of sanctification, their letter afforded but little encouragement.

While awaiting the reply of the Free Methodist conference, my brother had visited the Tennyson schoolhouse where we had held meetings sometime before. He found that no sect minister had yet demoralized the believers, and the members were more spiritual than those of any congregation we had yet visited. This occurrence threw some light on our difficulty. My brother, as was his usual custom when he had anything of great importance weighing on his mind, resorted to prayer. As it was March and the weather quite cool, he put on his overcoat and went out to spend the day alone until he got the leadings of the Lord.

God began to show him the sin of division. Jeremiah did not see matters very clearly yet, for he asked the Lord how we could get along without any human organization. The Lord asked him what good they had done, and brought to his mind the fact that it was only the spiritual ones, those who had not partaken of the spirit of division, that God could use to any advantage. My brother then inquired of the Lord how this sin of division had been brought about, and the Lord showed him that he could find the answer to his question in history.

When my brother had an opportunity to read history, he found that every sect builder told his own story. He saw that not one of the human organizations measured to the pattern of the New Testament church, and that since the sects have human founders, they could not be the church of God as that institution is of divine origin.

My brother then went back to the Tennyson school-house, and preached his first sermon on the subject of the unity of God's people. The people joyfully accepted the truth and walked in the light. Jeremiah thought that when I heard what God had revealed to him I would be rejoiced; but, to his surprise, I could not yet discern the body of Christ. I was still under the influence of the wine of Babylon.

Our meetings had been attended with excellent results. Many souls had sought the Lord. In one meeting, which lasted three or four weeks, the whole country was stirred. Many young men and even whole families got under deep conviction. After a day spent in fasting and prayer, we came together in the evening, and conviction settled so heavily upon the people and God worked so mightily that we labored at the altar until two o'clock in the morning. Almost every seat was an altar. Rain was falling, and the brush arbor in which the meeting was held did not protect the congregation; but the interest was so great that the seekers paid no attention to the water that constantly dripped through the boughs overhead. About twenty souls, I think, sought the Lord that night. During the whole series of meetings, a large number were saved.

About this time Sister Julia Meyers, now of Ima, New Mexico, joined our company, and for some months, traveled with us in the work. She had been healed before coming to us; but she got light on the one church in our meetings. The Lord had been teaching me to more fully trust him for temporal needs as well as for spiritual benefits. When Sister Meyers joined our company, I began to teach her the things that God had been showing me. I saw that she needed help. First she began borrowing money from me now and then to get what she needed. I felt that I should give her the money. Later, when I needed a pair of shoes, she began to feel that she should get them for me. She had enough money to buy the shoes, but found it a little difficult to obey the impression.

In the meantime I was earnestly praying for the shoes. God made me to understand that my prayer had gone through, and that I could have had the shoes sooner, had I prayed more earnestly. I was upstairs. It came to me, "How do you know but that the shoes are downstairs waiting for you?" In less than five minutes I was called downstairs; and, sure enough, there were the shoes. At first I did not know where they came from; but Sister Meyers was so blessed in her obedience and sacrifice that she could not keep her secret, and we praised the Lord together.

As I was preaching the straight gospel of salvation from sin, sanctification, and divine healing, it was to be expected that I should meet with opposition. I met with some very peculiar and unexpected persecutions. Falsehoods were told about me that should have shamed the devil himself. One rumor was that I was one of the famous outlaws, known as the "James Boys," disguised as a woman. One of the truth fighters published a long account of my meetings in the county newspaper. He branded me as an impostor, saying that I taught false doctrines. He affirmed that sanctification and divine healing were not for the people of the present day, that no one but Enoch and Elijah had been sanctified, both of whom went to heaven without dying. He ended his tirade against me by saying that I ought to be driven out of the country, and that he would join a mob raised for that purpose.

A Methodist lady, who no doubt had some understanding of Bible doctrine, replied to the gentleman with an article, in which she said that the Wesleys taught sanctification, and George Mueller, divine healing. "If," said she, "the gentleman would read more, he would be better informed. There is some hope yet for 'Tom Paine,'" referring to the fictitious name signed to his article. I did not know of this wordy battle until it was ended.

At times my brother would hold a meeting at one place and at the same time I would hold one a few miles distant. It was at one such time that I held a meeting in the county courthouse. I was assisted by a brother of the M. E. South denomination - a young college student, with but little experience in gospel work, thought that he could not preach unless he had his sermons written out. We preached on alternate evenings. One evening he came to me and said, "I wish you would occupy the pulpit tonight. I have been away and have had no chance for preparation." I told him that I had not had time for preparation either. "Sister Cole," he replied, "you can preach better without preparation than I can with preparation, besides, I haven't had my supper yet." "Perhaps you could preach better without supper," said I. Thus I held him to his duty and did not sympathize with him very much either. That night he had to lean so hard on God that many people said it was the best message they had ever heard him deliver.

Perhaps no young preacher going out in gospel work ever felt his inability more than I. As God had promised to be my sufficiency, I leaned hard upon him and did not feel discouraged. My education was so limited, that sometimes during a sermon, while trying to explain the Scriptures, I would lack words to express myself, and would look to the Lord, taking him as my wisdom. On such occasions he would supply me with words, and by his Spirit show me how to use them. Later, upon looking in the dictionary, I would find that they had been used correctly. This experience has been repeated many times in my ministry. Thus the Lord proved true his promise to be my spokesman. When I leaned on him, I was never confounded; no, not once. Truly our God is a covenant-keeping God, whom we can trust under all circumstances and at all times.

When the Lord healed me, he bestowed upon me the gift of exhortation and with it such a great measure of the Spirit's power that when I read the Scriptures, there was a heavenly illumination upon it, and I could see a sermon in almost every verse. At times the strength of this heavenly light so dazzled me that my mind and body were well-nigh overwhelmed. I studied and preached the Word under a light whose brightness could come only from the Spirit of the Lord, and I by spiritual sight could see through the Scriptures with a vision as unclouded as the vision before my natural eyes when looking through a clear glass. Oh, it was wonderful! I have always thought that God blessed me with this divine unfolding of the Scriptures because I did not at all depend upon my own human under-standing, but leaned wholly upon him at the very time that I was studying or expounding the Word. As I became accustomed to this heavenly light, I was not so much dazzled by its brilliancy, but the gift of exhortation with its accompaniment of divine power, has been mine, except for one brief time, throughout my ministry.

As I went from place to place preaching, I began to realize that I needed another gift of the Spirit - the gift of teaching. When the Lord first impressed me that he wanted me to teach, I begged off, saying that I stammered so that it was very hard for me to read. The Lord pitied me and took another plan to get me to do what he desired. Up to this time I had great freedom and much help in exhorting, but now God seemed to have taken this gift from me, and I became as one who had never had it. The Lord showed me that I would have to trust him for ability to teach and to explain the Word, and for help to overcome my stammering, or I would have no gift at all. So I got down and cried to him like a child and plead with him for help.

When the Lord saw that I was determined to obey him, he not only gave me the gift of teaching; but, to my surprise, he restored to me the gift of exhortation and let me exercise it as in days gone by. Surely the Lord humored me. I now had two gifts instead of one. But I would not advise others to do as I did, for though the Lord has no respect of person, you may have more light than I had at that time, and it may be that the Lord would not excuse you because of ignorance, as he excused me.

Quite early in my evangelistic work I held a meeting in a neighborhood where lived a man who had been an M. E. exhorter. He had once been saved, so the neighbors said, but having accepted a false doctrine that was being taught in that part of the country, and having partaken of its spirit, he was in a bad condition when I went there. He had rejected Christ entirely, saying that Jesus was nothing but an impostor.

Sometime before I went to the neighborhood, one of his children had gotten saved, and during the meeting that I held, another one had also come to Christ. Knowing their father's condition, the children feared his persecution and insisted that I should come and visit him. They thought that if I went to the house with them he would be more considerate. For their sakes, I went. I had heard that his practise was to invite ministers to his house, and then to belittle Christ in their presence, to give them no opportunity to return thanks, and to make them feel as far as possible his opposition to Christ.

After some conversation, he took down the Bible - the Old Testament I mean, he had no New Testament in the house - and told me that he was going to prove to me that Christ had never come. I told him that he could not do that, because by experience I knew that Christ had come. "If," said I, "you are going to try to prove to me that Christ has not come, you have gotten hold of the wrong person. I would stake my life that Christ has come. I have met the conditions prescribed in his Word, and he has given me the witness of my salvation, and has also healed me."

I tried in various ways to see if there was a tender spot in his heart that God could touch. Among other things, I said, "When I first started out in the work of the Lord, I wrote to my mother saying, 'I have found many good friends. All who are Jesus' friends,' I wrote, 'are my friends.' But," I continued, "I suppose I have now found a man who is not a friend of Jesus, and yet is my friend." I thought this would shame him. "Yes," he answered, "I am your friend, but not his." I returned thanks at the table and also asked him the privilege of praying before I left. The Spirit of God intimidated him till he did not dare to refuse me. Never did the name of Jesus seem half so sweet to me as when I got down to pray before this wicked man. It seemed as though all the sweetness of heaven was wrapped up in that name. I could say but little: I could only breathe out the precious name of Jesus; and oh, how he magnified himself through His name! Although I felt the presence of infernal spirits all around me - the very spirit that crucified Christ - yet I felt the presence, too, of the blessed Lord, the Christ of the Bible.

Still thinking that I might say something that would touch his heart, I said, as I was about to leave, "Pray for me." He said, "I will; and you pray for me: but not in the name of Jesus;" adding a moment later, "but I know that you will do as you please anyhow." I felt then that unless God directly ordered it, I never wanted to go again to a place where Christ was so entirely rejected. I thought of the scripture which says that they had forgotten that they were once purged. If ever I met a man who had sinned against the Holy Ghost, this was certainly the man.

In the early years of my ministry, I sometimes found that when the Lord was burdening my heart to preach on certain subjects my sympathy stood in the way; that is, I was afraid I would hurt somebody's feelings. One night I dreamed that another minister and I were standing near a large casket containing two dead bodies. It seemed that God wanted us to dissect these two bodies, and I said to the minister who was with me, "Brother, we had better get to work before the stench fills the room."

When I awoke I knew that God was trying to teach me something. Just a few days afterwards I went across the country accompanied by the brother, and his wife, of whom I had dreamed. Some of the congregation at the place where we were going to hold meeting on the next Sunday, were professing to be saved, and at the same time were living in adultery. Some others needed warning in regard to other sins. The Lord wanted me to preach to these people showing them where they stood;

but, because of my sympathy for them, I did not want
to handle the subject. The Lord reminded me that I had
promised to preach his Word on any subject. "Yes,
Lord," said I, "but I sympathize so with these people! I
would rather be whipped from head to foot than to
preach on this subject at this time." I preached, talking
first on one subject and then another, and not coming
to anything definite, entirely failing to give them that
portion of the Word that they so much needed.

That night I took very sick. It seemed that I should die.
I did not know what was the matter. I asked the Lord
why I was suffering so; and he reminded me that I had
said that I would rather be whipped from head to foot
than to preach on the subject he had given me, and that
now the whipping had come. When God administers
correction, he always does a thorough work. I begged
earnestly that he would take his hand off, promising
him faithfully that I would never grieve him in that
way any more; but I saw that I lacked sufficient Holy
Ghost boldness to carry out my decision if I continued
to sympathize with those for whom the message was
intended. So I asked the Lord earnestly for help, telling
him that if he wanted to use me in dissecting, he must
give me the ability. The lesson has never had to be
repeated.

During my earlier ministry an incident occurred which
to some might seem amusing; but which to me
furnished an excellent spiritual illustration. A class-
leader of the M. E. South denomination came a number
of miles across the country to take me to a certain
place to help in a meeting. We had to ford the
Gasconade river. It was winter, and the ice was frozen
thick. Before we reached the river, some men had cut a
road through the ice, so that people could cross on

horseback. As we rode out into the stream the flowing water seemed to affect me strangely. It seemed to me that the brother who was with me was trying to pull me off of the horse and drown me. I said, "Don't, don't, it is all I can do to stay on now." When we reached the other side, the brother broke into a hearty laugh: "Sister Cole, did you think I was trying to drown you? I saw that the water made you dizzy, and that you were about to fall off the horse. It was all I could do to keep you from drowning."

Many times since then I have thought of this incident, as an illustration of a certain spiritual condition. When a person gets somewhat cold spiritually, the doctrines of the church become indistinct, and, spiritually speaking, his head begins to swim. At such a time he is likely to think that those who are endeavoring to help him out of his difficulties are trying to drown him; that they are in spiritual trouble themselves and that they are trying to pull him into the same difficulty.

At another time I was going to a meeting near the place of which I have just told you, and had to cross the same river. It was earlier in the fall; and the Gasconade, although badly swollen, had not yet frozen. The boy who was with me, feared that the river was too high for fording, and asked what we should do. As the appointment had already been made for me, I feared that the people would be disappointed and told him we would better go across if we could. "Shall I go across first and see how deep the water is?" he asked. I told him I thought that would be the better way. He found the water to be deep enough to swim our horses, but thought that we might get across, although we would risk our lives in the attempt. He said that if I wanted to run the risk, he was willing. God protected us and we reached the other side in safety.

The young man said to some of his friends afterwards, that he was afraid we would both drown, but that he would not let a woman back him out. "I knew," said he "that if she drowned, she would be saved; but that if I drowned, I should be lost." I certainly appreciated his generosity in risking his life to help me.

While holding meetings in that neighborhood, this same young man and his brother, although unsaved, befriended me in every way possible, because they knew that I had come there to do the people good. Their sisters, who professed religion, also manifested great friendliness for me. At one time when some sectarian holiness fighters tried to shut me out of the schoolhouse, the two brothers defended me like lawyers, won the case, and secured the use of the house for as long as I desired to hold meetings. Whenever I needed a conveyance, I had only to call on these young men.

I met a brother young in the ministry who had a very clear definite experience of justification and sanctification, and who had had a very definite call. He had had, however, but very little experience in tests and trials, and was therefore not qualified to be the blessing to young converts or to young workers that he might have been. As he had been so victorious in his religious experience, he thought that trials and tests were a sign of weakness, and that those who had them were spiritual weaklings. Whenever a young convert or worker had a test or a trial of faith, and needed special help or encouragement, he would think, "Oh, well it isn't worth while to bother with him; he doesn't amount to much anyway. He will not stand, and if he does, he won't ever be very useful in the Lord's cause. He is not worthy of any attention."

God let this brother go through deep waters. He had a severe test; and when he came through, his compassion was much increased, and his care and consideration for the young converts and those in trouble was all that could be desired. He did not find any one then unworthy his consideration. He had learned that every soul worth Christ's dying for, is worth all the effort we can make, either for its deliverance or its establishment. Well did the Psalmist say, "When I was in trouble thou hast enlarged my steps." The Psalmist got the enlargement right in the trial, just as we often do. Much of our development is obtained in the furnace of trial; in fact, I believe most of it. Let us be thankful, therefore, for the dispensation of God's grace, whether it be bestowed by trial or in sunshine; whether it comes in storm or in calm, knowing that God allows all for our highest good.

Quite early in our evangelistic labors my brother saw that I had been leaning too much on him. Frequently when God wanted me to deliver a message, I would hold back and let my brother preach instead. I was not getting the experience I should, nor being as useful in the Lord's work as I might. My brother thought that if he should leave me to work alone for a time, the Lord would have a chance to help me more. He therefore began leaving me to hold meetings alone for weeks at a time, while he held services in some nearby neighborhood. Naturally, I felt somewhat fearful about being left to carry on the work alone; but the Lord helped me and enabled me to hold a number of good successful meetings.

At one of these meetings God had been answering prayer and conviction was falling heavily upon the people. The whole neighborhood seemed stirred, and crowds were at the altar. Fathers and mothers came seeking salvation. A few, however, among them a Campbellite minister, came with the intention of causing trouble. He wanted a chance, he said to tell the people how to find Jesus. I asked him what he would tell them. "Obey the commendments." "What commandments?" "Join the church and be baptized." "If you have a message from God," said I, "we will hear it; but, if you have not, we will not hear it. Souls are at the altar and their eternal interests are at stake. This is too serious a time to deliver a message not from God." He arose and went out, accompanied by the man who had come with him. When the sinners laughed at him, he said, "If you had had such hot testimonies thrown into your faces, you would have left too." When this same minister came to another meeting to disturb, God got hold of him and brought him to the altar. I don't think he got an experience, but he made no more attempts to disturb the meeting.

Every time the enemy undertook to hinder the work, God marvelously helped us. At one time a certain minister came to try to look me out of countenance while I was preaching. His plan was to confuse me so that I could not preach. The enemy knew that if I became the least bit confused, I would stammer so that I could hardly talk. God was present to help me. He so confounded the man that before the service was over, his head went down and I had no more trouble with him.

At different times I held meetings of three or four week's duration, preaching twice every day and three times on Sunday. I had no help in the preaching, and but very little at the altar service. There were many people at the altar seeking God and the work was very heavy. The Lord wonderfully sustained me. The fact that I went through such fatiguing experiences as these, laboring sometimes far into the night, shows how wonderfully God had healed me, and how he was sustaining me in my work.

Experience alone will show how much the dear Lord can help us physically as well as spiritually if we but trust him. Unbelief and doubts hinder God from being to us our sufficiency at all times and under all circumstances. Faith will take hold of God for things beyond the comprehension of our natural minds. The Word says, "All things are possible with God"; "All things are possible to him that believeth." As we trust in the Lord, he will honor our faith and give us the desire of our hearts.

Chapter XII

Out of Sectarian Confusion

I was still a Methodist. The Methodist did not license women to preach; but when the preachers found out that God was using me in the salvation of souls and that I was not especially interested in building up any certain denomination, I had an abundance of calls.

God had already begun talking to my brother Jeremiah about the sin of division, and he was beginning to see the evils of sectarianism. The winter after I was healed, he had attended the Jacksonville, Illinois, holiness convention, and had met there Bro. D. S. Warner, who at that time was editor of a holiness paper, *The Herald of Gospel Freedom*, then published at Rome City, Ind. Brother Warner was already beginning to discern the unity of God's people, but he had not yet received enough light on the subject to sever his connection with the Winebrennerian denomination, of which he was a member. It was about the time of the Jacksonville meeting that *The Herald of Gospel Freedom* was consolidated with *The Pilgrim*, a small holiness paper published at Indianapolis, Indiana.

While at the Jacksonville meeting, Jeremiah subscribed for *The Pilgrim* and had it sent to me at Windsor, Missouri, as I had not yet begun gospel work.

I received only a few numbers of *The Pilgrim*, as that publication was consolidated with *The Herald of Gospel Freedom* January 1, 1881, under the name *The Gospel Trumpet*. At a later date, when Brother Warner had full light on the church, *The Gospel Trumpet* was no longer considered a consolidation of the two papers, but an entirely new publication. The first issue of *The Trumpet* (January 1, 1881) represented a new paper and was later designated as Vol. 1, No. 1. When the publication of *The Pilgrim* ceased, Brother Warner began to send me *The Gospel Trumpet* to finish out the unexpired time of my subscription to *The Pilgrim*.

During my brother's absence in evangelistic work I received several copies of *The Trumpet*. As soon as I read in *The Trumpet* about the sin of division and saw that the new paper opposed the licensing of preachers, my sectarian spirit was stirred. I thought that holiness would make the churches, as I called them, better. I was afraid that if people got hold of such literature as *The Trumpet* it would disgust them with holiness forever. I burned *The Trumpets* I had already received, and then sat down and wrote Brother Warner never to send me another copy. As I was traditionized, and had opposed the truth in ignorance, the Lord did not hold my opposition as a wilful sin.

After my brother had got light on the one body, he was so enthused with the truth that he wanted to explain it to every one he met. While out walking one day the next summer after he discerned the one body, he fell into conversation with a man about the Scriptures. After talking a little while the man said, "I have a paper that reads just as you talk." Going to the house, he brought out *The Gospel Trumpet* and gave it to my brother, who went down the road reading as he went.

He never stopped reading until he had finished the paper. At the earliest opportunity my brother wrote a letter to Brother Warner, asking him if he had enough light on the one body to set it clearly before the people. He also asked him if many were accepting this divine truth. To the first question Brother Warner replied, "Yes," and to the second, "Yes, hundreds are discerning the one body." As soon as my brother learned that Brother Warner and many others had the same truth that God had made so clear and beautiful to him, he rejoiced greatly. He could not rest until he went where Brother Warner was; but, as I had neglected to walk in the light, I was left alone, and that, too, in more ways than one.

Some time before I discerned the body of Christ, I had some impressive dreams. In one I thought I was in a large building belonging to some denomination. A conference of that denomination was being held just outside the door, and the ministers wanted me to come and take part. I looked toward the door through which I must pass, and I saw two large worms with their heads together, lying directly across the threshold. In order to enter the room, I would have to step over the worms and would be in great danger of receiving a deadly bite. I said to myself, "I will not run the risk for any man's notions or ways"; and, turning on my heel, I went out of another door.

I soon saw my dream fulfilled. The denomination that I had been holding a meeting for insisted that I should join their conference, saying that they would give me a license so that I could hold meetings in their territory. I knew that, according to their discipline, they could not license a woman to preach; and I said to the minister, "You don't dare to give me a license." "Well," said he,

Mary Cole

"I will tell you what you can do, Sister Cole; we can go to a place not far from here where you have had a good meeting, lay this matter before the people, and have them vote to give you a permit, so that you can hold meetings in any part of our district." I did not feel at all led to take such steps; and, as I had done in my dream, I turned in the other direction. I suppose God was using this method to get me ready for the truth.

The summer before I got out of sectarianism, an M. E. South minister invited me to come to their new chapel, to attend the quarterly conference, and to help hold a series of meetings. As the M. E. South denomination did not license women preachers, women were not allowed at the quarterly conference. They had arranged, however, that several other women and I should sit in a room adjoining the conference, so that we could hear the proceedings. This was on Saturday. On Sunday morning they held their quarterly love-feast, partook of the Lord's Supper, and listened to a sermon by the presiding elder.

In the afternoon and the evening, I preached. While the afternoon service was in progress, the ministers were holding a private meeting to decide whether or not I should proceed with the meeting I had come to hold. In this part of the country was a wealthy man, a sinner, who contributed very liberally to the support of the work. This man objected to women's preaching and opposed the continuance of the meeting.

It was decided that the meeting should not continue, but the pastor of the congregation did not tell me. The pastor and his wife were both present at the service on Monday night, and both seemed well pleased. On Tuesday evening the interest began to increase, and one or two raised their hands for prayer. Just at the close of the service a note was handed me requesting me to close the meeting, as they had decided not to continue at the present time, but to wait until later in the season.

I could not keep from crying. I had called the Methodist Church my mother; and now to think that my mother was treating me in this way, made me feel very bad. I went home with a young couple who had been saved a short time before in a meeting held near this place. They felt very bad over what had happened, and we all cried together. The young people tried to encourage me as best they could.

Next day they took me to their aunt's, a special friend of mine, who had shown me kindness while I was in that neighborhood before. As we went along the road, I thought to myself, "Any one treated as I have been ought to look sneaking"; and I tried to think of everything I could to make me look that way. When we arrived at our destination, the sister was not in the room, so I hunted the smallest chair I could find, and sat down. As soon as she came in, she saw that I was in trouble and inquired what was the matter. I began to tell her, crying at the same time; but she began to laugh. Well, she laughed and I cried; but after a while I took to laughing too. I never again felt bad about my treatment at that place.

I still continued to get calls from the sectarian preachers to go and help hold meetings. I responded to these, and held two or three meetings in different places. Late that fall I held a meeting at Rolla, Mo. The preacher could hardly get an audience when he preached, so he sent for me, thinking that a woman preacher would be quite an attraction and would draw crowds. The crowds came. Although there were a number of ministers present, including the presiding elder, I occupied the pulpit, I think, during half of that meeting. Conviction came upon the people, and a number came to the altar; but not many of those who came, seemed to get an experience.

On the last night of the meeting quite a number of bright, intelligent young people, some of them college students came to the altar and some of them were getting saved. As the minister went to talk with the seekers one by one, God put it into my heart to listen to what they were saying. Not once did these preachers say, "Seek the Lord until you find him;" "There is reality in salvation;" "Never stop until you know you are saved." Their instructions were: "Join the church;" "Get baptized," etc. God opened my eyes right there to the awful work that these so-called ministers were doing. I said, "If they are going to help deceive souls that way and send them to destruction, I will never help them again." That was the last meeting in which I ever helped to build up Babylon.

Collections were taken up for the ministers and for the general expenses of the meeting, but no one ever said to me, "Do you need any means?" One of the sisters, however, found out that I had a little money, and she asked me to give it to her to use in buying a little clothing for me so I would be suitably dressed to preach in their meeting. I felt that even this was too good for me, because I had failed to walk in the light.

At the close of the meeting, to my surprise, I found myself under a wrong spirit. I went to Bro. John P. Bailey and wife, who had accepted the truth when

Jeremiah preached his first sermon on the church at that place. I told Brother and Sister Bailey my condition as best I could, and the three of us fasted and prayed three days. God delivered me from the false spirit, gave me light on the one body, the church, and made me glad to walk in the light as fast as it was revealed.

Bro. Jake Cruts came to ask my advice on the subject of baptism. "Sister Cole," said he, "what do you think about baptism: is it a commandment of God? If so, what is the correct mode?" Before I could answer him, he continued, "I suppose we shall never know the right mode." "I believe," said I, "if we are sincere and come to God in earnest prayer, he will show us his will, even if the scripture on that doctrine has been wrongly translated." The brother agreed with me, and I said, "Let us get down and pray." While we were on our knees, God made me to understand that in the near future, he would make known to me his will on the subject of baptism.

I told the brother who was kneeling with me what God had shown me; but it seemed that I needed to be humbled still more. At this time I received another *Trumpet* in which there was an article by D. S. Warner on the subject of baptism. I said to myself, "He is nothing but a Baptist preacher anyway," and found myself going into gross darkness. For about two hours it seemed that I was bound for hell. I cried out, "O Lord! why is it that after you have used me in the salvation of souls, some of whom no doubt are in the glory-world, I must now be lost?" The Lord made me understand that I was not responsible for not having been baptized, as I had no knowledge of the teaching of the Scriptures on this subject, but that I was responsible for my present light. He showed me that, if I would walk in the light, I should not be lost. I decided then and there to walk in every ray of light that God gave me.

As members of the M. E. Church, my parents had had me sprinkled when I was a child, and up to this time I had had no light on baptism. When I had opportunity and I was buried in baptism, God wonderfully witnessed that I was being baptized in his order.

My first text after I got light on the one body of Christ, was Jeremiah 1:6-10 and 17-19. A short time before this I had held a meeting with an M. E. South preacher, who now seemed to stand before me like an obstructing mountain. As I began my sermon, I seemed to see him in that capacity. Before I was through delivering the message, however, God had lifted me above the mountain, so that I was never again troubled in that way.

My name was still on the M. E. class-book; but God showed me that I ought to have it removed, and how to have it removed. I sent for my church letter and trusted the Lord to direct me how to dispose of it. One Sunday after a sermon had been delivered on the church of God, I rose and told the congregation about the church letter, told them that the Lord had shown me that I could not have two valid contracts for my entire service with two different parties at the same time. I said, "I have decided that the contract between God and my soul is the more important one." Then I proceeded to tear up my letter, and God sent his mighty power, witnessing that my contract with the Lord was ratified in heaven. So much of heaven came down, and the glory world seemed so near, that I seemed attached to heaven, not by a cord, but by a mighty cable. I shall never be able to express how satisfied I was with God's church. Some sectarian preachers prophesied that I should soon be back preaching for the denominations. One of them was heard to say, "If I knew that Mary Cole would come and help us in a meeting, I would send for her; but I am afraid she won't." I never got any more special calls from Babylon.

Shortly after I got light on the one body, however, the devil laid a snare for me. I saw the snare before I got into it, and God's Word was fulfilled: "In vain is the net spread in the sight of any bird." It happened in this way: A certain man who was starting a new sect tried to interest all he could in his project. He did not call his new religious movement by any special name and professed not to have anything to join. He would have the people come and shake hands, inferring that in so doing they were not joining anything, but were merely showing their mutual love and fellowship. In order to be an encouragement to any that might really be trying to live for the Lord, I went up and shook hands with the preacher and others. After we had shaken hands, his design became apparent. He seated me and a few others on one side of the platform and called for others to come and shake hands with us. The Lion of the tribe of Judah began to roar in my soul. I got up very quickly, and the plan was defeated.

A common remark made to me by sectarians was, "You ought to join some denomination so that you will be inside the pale of the church," thus inferring that because I did not belong to a human organization, I was not in good pasture, but outside on the commons with poor, ill-fed stock. I understood the figure of speech very well, for I was brought up on a farm where the garden was enclosed with palings. Between these palings were spaces through which small animals could get in and destroy the vegetables - a very good illustration of the sectarian churches surrounded by their palings, through which unclean spirits can slip in and destroy the flock. In the church of God I feel secure; because God has appointed salvation for her walls and bulwarks (Isaiah 26:1), and through these neither evil spirits, nor even the devil himself can penetrate.

I was educated to believe, and in this way I often expressed myself, that the M. E. denomination was my spiritual mother. This idea remained with me until I got light on the sin of division and was spiritually able to discern the bride of Christ. Then I saw that "Jerusalem from above is the mother of us all." I saw plainly that if I had two mothers, one must be a stepmother. While my mother was living I never cared to have a stepmother. The prophecies of Scripture so unmistakably point to the one church, the body of Christ, that they can be but poorly explained by those who are trying to make them conform to sectarian theology. I am content with the church of God, with Christ as the door, and nothing inside but the holy throng.

Besides, in sectarianism I did not have freedom in my ministry. I could preach only as the sect ministers suggested. If God gave me more light, and I tried to give it to the people, I was likely to receive a rebuke. I remember that at one time while I was holding a meeting for some denomination, God led me to preach on holiness. In the very beginning of the meeting they had advised me not to preach on this subject. What was

I to do? The Lord reminded that I had promised I would preach any part of his Word whenever and wherever he led me to do so. He now brought me face to face with the question, "What will you do?" I said, "Lord, I will obey you if you will stand by me." The Lord assured me that he would. I preached on sanctification as a distinct second work of grace, God witnessing to the message by his mighty power. After the service, the minister who had placed the restrictions upon me, said, "Sister Cole, that is the best sermon you preached during the whole meeting." I answered, "I knew that the things you didn't want were the things you needed."

After the Lord had led me into the precious truth of the oneness of his people, I was much better satisfied with what God did with me and through me, with the meetings I held, and with the results attained. Although at times not as many people professed salvation now as when I was preaching for the denomination, yet those who got saved reached a settled experience, being satisfied that they were in God's order. They were not looking around for something that more nearly represented the truth. As a minister I was satisfied, knowing that I was delivering the whole counsel of God. No one ever can be satisfied who is not walking in every ray of light that God turns on his pathway.

Chapter XIII

The Evening Light

This chapter is an article written by the author many years after she had received light on the unity of the church. It will acquaint the reader with what is meant by the expression "evening light."

"At evening time it shall be light."

"And it shall come to pass in that day, that the light shall not be clear, nor dark: but it shall be one day which shall be known to the Lord, not day, nor night: but it shall come to pass, that at evening time it shall be light" (Zechariah 14:6,7). The expression "evening light" suggests the thought that there was at one time morning light. The New Testament dispensation is sometimes called the gospel day. Like the natural day, this gospel day has its morning and evening.

When the New Testament church was first set in order; when this Holy Ghost dispensation was ushered in; when the gospel day began there was a wonderful outburst of light and power from the glory-world. "The people which sat in darkness saw great light; and to them which sat in the region and shadow of death light is sprung up" (Matthew 4:16). As a result of this mighty flood of power and light, the place where the saints were assembled was shaken (Acts 2:1-7), the dead were raised to life, the blind were made to see, the deaf to hear, the dumb to speak the lame to walk, all manner of diseases were healed, thousands upon thousands were converted to God, and many signs and wonders were wrought in the name of the holy child Jesus. We also read of Paul's wonderful conversion, of Peter's deliverance from prison, and of many who were delivered from devils. Oh, what wonderful light God shed upon the hearts of men at that time!

The shining of this glorious light not only enlightened the minds of those who received it; but it also revealed the effects of past traditions and brushed them away. The light also revealed the New Testament life and experience, far exceeding the standard under the law. The word says, "Light makes manifest"; so under the gospel rays every one's condition was revealed. The light not only showed the people their sins, but also showed them how to get rid of them, and then how later to get sanctified wholly. "For this is the will of God, even your sanctification" (1 Thesselonians 4:3).

This, of course, is a much higher standard than was raised under the law. The law was, eye for eye, tooth for tooth, love your neighbor and hate your enemy; but when the gospel light revealed God's will in this dispensation, all people became so responsible because of the knowledge of divine truth revealed to them and the unmeasured divine power bestowed upon them that it was consistent to raise the standard where people would love their enemies and do good to those who despitefully treated them. Nor did their love stop with that; it so increased toward one another that "all that believed were together, and had all things common; and sold their possessions and goods, and parted them to all men, as every man had need" (Acts 2:44,45).

In many particulars far too numerous to mention can it be shown that the New Testament standard was raised far above the law standard, showing God's compassion to fallen man. For example, consider the woman taken in adultery. The law said, "Stone her to death"; but Jesus said, "Neither do I condemn thee; go and sin no more." Notice also his compassion toward the Syrophenician woman, who was considered a Gentile dog; toward the people when he performed the miracles of the loaves and fishes; toward the multitude when he fed enemies as well as friends. Again, when the disciples wanted to call down fire from heaven to destroy some who had opposed them, Jesus said, "I am not come to destroy men's lives, but to save them." Jesus loved the people so well that he healed even the man in the tombs who was possessed with a legion of devils, and also the ear of the servant of the high priest who was then helping to arrest him. It was his compassion that sent out the disciples to heal the sick, to raise the dead, and to cast out devils. All these things were a result of the burning light that shone forth in the morning of this gospel day.

We see that God's church in the beginning was a mighty moving power - a means in God's hands to bring deliverance and salvation to souls, and healing to afflicted bodies. The work done and the signs wrought all so far exceeded what had been done before that the people were made to exclaim, "We never saw it on this fashion." Jesus summed it up well when he said, "The blind received their sight, and the lame walk, the lepers are cleansed, and the deaf hear, the dead are raised up, and the poor have the gospel preached to them. And blessed is he whosoever shall not be offended in me"

(Matthew 11:5,6). If from the morning time until now the light had continued to shine with unclouded brightness, who knows how much might have been done toward the salvation of the world! But, alas! the prophecy must needs be fulfilled: "And it shall come to pass in that day, saith the Lord God, that I will cause the sun to go down at noon, and I will darken the earth in the clear day" (Amos 8:9). In Paul's time he said, "For the mystery of iniquity doth already work" (2 Thessalonians 2:7).

It was not long until the people began to drift away from God, to substitute outward form for inward experience, and penance for faith. Heresies sprang up. Men lost sight of the church of God, and began to form creeds, and to build up man-made institutions. The first creed was formed in A. D.

325. Men drifted farther and farther away from the way of the Lord, and plunged into gross darkness, until they could even kill the saints and think they were doing God's service. They also fell to worshiping images after the manner of the heathen, and doing many other like things. This departure from light brought about a serious state of affairs; so great was the persecution of God's true children that they were hunted for their lives, and had to hide in dens and caves of the earth. History tells us that death was the penalty for having in possession a New Testament. With such a penalty hanging over the people of God, not many would be professing that did not have the experience. It doubtless took a martyr's consecration to keep a real Christian experience in those days, and it is equally as much needed in these perilous times.

This reign of gross darkness continued hundreds of

years. "Behold, the days come, saith the Lord God, that I will send a famine in the land, not a famine of bread, nor thirst for water, but of hearing the words of the Lord" (Amos 8:11). But God had designed to bring again his children out of darkness. He proceeded to do so by giving light to such men as Wycliffe, Huss, Luther, and others. History tells us that when light came to Luther, he was steeped in Catholicism, so much so that he was trying to gain favor with God by various acts of penance. On one occasion while he was climbing the "holy stairs" at Rome on his hands and knees, the Lord thundered in his soul that salvation is by faith in Christ alone. We have no account of Luther's getting light beyond justification, but the reformation did not cease with him. Later the Lord gave to the Wesleys, Fletcher, Hester Ann Rogers, and others, greater light on his Word, showing the privilege not only of justification but also of sanctification. As the departure from the light and whole truth in the morning of the gospel day was a gradual process, so the return to the light has been gradual. The Lord shed some light on the world through Huss, some through Luther, and some through the Wesleys and others, thus restoring the full light according to his own plan.

While God wonderfully used these men to shed light on the world in their day, yet many effects of the apostasy were clinging to them. Divine healing in their day was almost unknown or known to but few, and likewise the gifts of the Spirit. Wesley himself testified that he did not possess any of the gifts of the Spirit, and did not think that any one else did. No one in Wesley's time, so far as we know, discerned the one body and the unity of God's children. The one who perhaps came nearest to discerning the body of Christ was either Wesley or Fletcher. In their correspondence with each other, one said in substance the following: "In searching the Word on the unity of God's children, I see that the Scriptures relating to the gathering of God's children into one body must be fulfilled before the end; but I scarcely think we are yet on the threshold of that period." He expressed his desire to see that time by saying, "God hasten the day." No doubt if these men were living today, and walking in the light as they were at that time, they would readily fall into line with the church in this evening time.

"At evening time it shall be light." That this scripture might be fulfilled, God in his wisdom saw fit to shed more light on the one body and divine healing, not upon one person alone, but upon a number of his people in different parts of the world. This light began to break forth about 1880. I wish to call your attention here to the way in which God shed forth the light on the church of God. In making a new sect, some man becomes the hub and center, and round him or his ideas revolves the organization. But God did not center this reform in one man, but gave the light to different ones in various parts of the world about the same time. The work of the Holy Spirit upon their hearts in sanctifying them, caused them to see and flow together. It might be said that the giving of this glorious light was in one respect similar to the second coming of the Son of man: "As the lightning cometh out of the east, and shineth even unto the west; so shall also the coming of the Son of man be." The fact that many persons in different parts of the world saw this light independently of each other and at about the same time is one evidence that this movement is God's work and not man's. Truly this is the evening time, and it is light.

God's will, order, and plan are more fully revealed to his children now than at any other time since the days of the apostles. The Lord enables us more clearly to discern the one body and its operations, and to know our place in it. The gifts of the Spirit are now recognized as belonging rightfully to God's children, and are sought, obtained and used to the glory of God. It is now understood that the same purity of heart and life enjoined by the church in the morning time is not only our privilege to enjoy, but also the standard to which we must measure, and the doctrine that we as ministers must both live and preach. The old Babylon doctrine, "Sin you must," is exposed as a doctrine of devils. The doctrine and practise of trusting the Lord for healing and at the same time using drugs and remedies to help the Lord out is cast aside as false, and the true doctrine of entire trust in God for healing is taught and practised instead. Truly the prophecy is fulfilled which says, "The light of the moon shall be as the light of the sun, and the light of the sun shall be sevenfold" (Isaiah 30:26).

At the same time that God is shedding more light on his Word, his plan, and his holy bride, he is also giving us more light on the workings of Satan and his deceptive power. As the light shines brighter, of course the battle waxes hotter between God and the devil, between light and darkness. As the light reveals the hiding-places of the devil and exposes his works, he is becoming more and more enraged and is making a desperate fight, for his time is short. This means much to the true saints in these perilous times. The enemy is not only doing all he can to hold those who are already under his power, but is doing all he can to spot the pure bride. Since he already sways his scepter over the sectarian world, he needs waste no time on them, but can direct all his energies against the holy remnant.

The harder Satan works, however, the brighter shines the church of God, the one body, the bride of Christ, the more glorious her splendor and beauty. Let us beware. Let us watch and pray, that we may be kept pure and clean. The Lord is the same today as ever, and his promises are as far-reaching. While it takes more grace to live a holy life at this time, yet the dear Lord has provided a sufficiency. As a result we have more to enjoy, and more facilities for doing good. The heavier the responsibilities, the greater the grace.

It is a thing indeed to be thankful for, that instead of the reign of conferences and synods, priests and popes, we have the blessed privilege of living under the loving rule of the holy Trinity, with Christ himself as the head of the church, and all we are breth-ren. "And I heard as it were the voice of a great multitude, and as the voice of many waters, and as the voice of mighty thunderings, saying Alleluia; for the Lord God omnipotent reigneth" (Revelation 19:6)

Truly we are highly favored among men. While we are now living in a time of great spiritual peril, and have to encounter many dangers by the way, yet we have more to enjoy, and God is more perfectly revealing himself now, than at any other time since the apostles.

> "Brighter days are sweetly dawning,
> Oh, the glory looms in sight!
> For the cloudy day is waning,
> And the ev'ning shall be light.
>
> "Misty fogs, so long concealing
> All the hills of mingled night,

Vanish, all their sin revealing,
For the ev'ning shall be light.

"Oh, what golden glory streaming!
Purer light is coming fast;
Now in Christ we've found a freedom,
Which eternally shall last."

Do you not think we should be very thankful since we are the most highly favored people on earth? "And let the peace of God rule in your hearts, to the which also ye are called in one body; and be ye thankful" (Colossians 3:15). Those of us who have been delivered from the dark night of Babylon confusion, and translated into this glorious light, surely have every kind of reason for which to be thankful. Therefore "let us be glad and rejoice, and give honor to him: for the marriage of the Lamb is come, and his wife hath made herself ready" (Revelation 19:7). "And the kingdom and dominion, and the greatness of the kingdom under the whole heaven, shall be given to the people of the saints of the Most High, whose kingdom is an everlasting kingdom, and all dominions shall serve and obey him" (Daniel 7:27). Read Daniel 7:15-28.

Chapter XIV

Various Experiences in Gospel Work

Soon after I discerned the one body, my brother and I visited St. James, Mo. We had labored there but a short time when Brother Warner and his company came to the town to hold a camp-meeting. When I was first introduced to Brother Warner, he made the remark, "And so you are the sister that wanted to stay in Babylon in order to get wolves to take care of lambs?" and then broke into a hearty laugh. He referred to my remark that I was going to continue to work with the sects, so that whenever a congregation was raised up I could get a sectarian minister to serve as pastor. I enjoyed Brother Warner's merriment, as I was free from sectarian bondage. He was truly a man of God; as meek, humble, and Christlike as any one I have ever met. Meeting him seemed very much like meeting Jesus himself, He was always ready to comfort and encourage young workers. He once felt so bad over having neglected to pray for a sister that was suffering, that he went to the altar and sought forgiveness, although his neglect had been due to the fact that he was so busy that he could scarcely have done otherwise than he did.

Before I began traveling with my brother, he had labored at St. James, where quite a company of saints was raised up. When we visited the town together, strange things were happening. The members of the congregation were having peculiar manifestations in their services - jumping, dancing, and doing other strange things, which they did not know whether to attribute to God or the devil, but which they thought were of the Lord.

My experience at this time showed that I was not entirely free from the influence of the traditions that I had received when a child. In my early years I had been instructed that different bodily demonstrations, such as dancing, jumping, etc., which occurred in the sect meetings some fifty years before, were all of God. When, therefore, we visited this little town, we accepted all their demonstrations as being of God. I even let some who were possessed with devils lay hands on me. I became affected with their false spirit, and on certain occasions my joints would become stiff and I would fall in a trance.

About this time Brother Warner and his company came to the town to hold a camp-meeting. As I went to shake hands with Mother Smith, who was with them at that time, I fell stiff. Mother Smith knew what was the matter at once. At first Brother Warner was somewhat puzzled, as he could see that although some of us were affected by this false spirit, we still had the spirit of God. As he wanted to be sure of every step he took, he began to work very carefully, holding on to God for guidance.

Finally God showed him that the time had come to send forth judgment. He read the 12th, 13th, and 14th chapters of I Corinthians. He said he was going to give us a big gospel dish at this time, and when he came to the scripture, "Charity does not behave itself unseemly," the judgments went forth in mighty torrents.

I was sitting in the congregation, knowing that I had some of the devil's chatties on me. At first I thought I would go out and pray it through; then I said, "No, I will look to God right here where I am." I raised my hand to God and said, "Lord, you must show me what is of God and what is not, so I can take my stand for you." Before my hand went down, God made me to know that Brother Warner and his company were right, and that the judgments going forth were of the Lord. I took my stand for the truth.

At this time and place it meant much to stand for the truth, for the whole country was polluted with this false spirit, and when judgment went forth, it stirred up the enemy throughout the whole country. As a result, a mob came that night after the services were ended, tore up the tents, and loaded everybody and everything connected with the meeting onto wagons and quietly sent them off the camp-ground. I was staying that night at a house about two miles from the camp-ground, and so was not present when the mob came. About two o'clock in the morning Brother Warner, who had got separated from his company, came, with a number of others, to the house where I was staying. I was awakened very early in the morning to pray for a brother's child that was sick. I did not feel clear to do this alone, as I had not sufficient victory over the recent attack of the enemy. Finding out that Brother Warner was there, I called him. We laid hands on the child, prayed for it, and it was healed.

Then I had them lay hands on me and pray that all the

bad effects of the recent attack of the enemy might be overcome. There was still a stir all through the country, and soon the people began to gather at the house where we were staying. Many of them were now able to see that they had been under the influence of wicked spirits, and desired deliverance. So many came that from the time we had our breakfast in the morning until the sun went down at night, we stopped neither to eat nor to rest, but were continually in prayer for those who wanted help.

It had been the design of the mob to kill Brother Warner, but the Lord graciously delivered him. It was the second day after the mob came, before Brother Warner found his company; he and they had gone in different directions. In the days following, Mother Smith was quite helpful to me, as the enemy tried to depress and crush me; but the Lord brought me off more than conqueror. A number of other honest souls were also gloriously delivered at this time; some of whom are New Testament ministers today.

God soon showed me that I must trust him for heavenly authority over devils and over every foul spirit. I came to God in earnest prayer, claimed my privilege as a minister, and obtained the gift of miracles. I soon had an opportunity to exercise the gift.

The following spring, in company with my brother, I had the privilege of attending the Bangor, Michigan, camp-meeting. For sometime I had felt the leadings of the Lord to go to this meeting, but I did not have the means. I began praying earnestly that God would open the way for me to go, but he saw fit to let my faith be tested. The time of the meeting was drawing near, and the money for my trip did not seem to be forthcoming.

As the time approached and different people asked me if I was going, I would say yes. Some would ask me if I had the means for my car-fare, to which I would answer no. "Well," said they, "what will you do if God does not give you the means?" I replied, "I will trust him anyway." Soon, however, the Lord showed me that I should begin fasting and praying, and that I should not eat until the money was provided. Breakfast on Saturday morning was my last meal until the following Monday morning. By that time God had answered my prayer: I had enough money to take me to the meeting, and there was a little left to apply on my return fare.

It is unnecessary for me to say that I enjoyed this my first meeting after getting victory over my sectarian blindness, past traditions, etc. The meeting was certainly precious and heavenly. The songs were so sweet, being sung in the spirit, and having such a heavenly melody. It seemed, almost, that I was where angels had congregated. Brother Warner would leap, shout, and praise the Lord, both in meeting and between meetings when he would meet a saint. Whenever a new saint came on the ground, you would hear shouts, praises, and halleluiahs, that would make the woods ring. In the morning when we first met each other, our salutations were, "Praise the Lord!" "The Lord bless you!" etc. I have heard Brother Warner say when he met those who seemed to have no praises stirring in their souls, "Have you no calves this morning?" referring to the scripture, "We should offer the calves of our lips, even praises to our God." I have been present when, under the anointing of the Spirit, Brother Warner preached three hours and twenty-five minutes; and those that were interested were not the least bit tired. While my brother and I were attending a camp-meeting at Chanute, Kansas, our systems got filled with malaria. Coming back to the home of Father Bolds, near Webb City, Missouri, I soon came down with typhoid fever. My brother had an attack, also; but, as he fought it more successfully than I, he soon recovered. I had a fight of faith. It seemed difficult for me to get hold of the Lord for healing. On examining my consecration, I found that I was more anxious to die than to live. When I got that difficulty out of the way, the Lord soon raised me up.

Nevertheless, I lay three and one-half weeks, most of the time with my tongue swelled stiff in my mouth. I could eat no solid food, not even softened bread. During that time I lived on liquid foods, such as grape juice and buttermilk. Prayer had been offered for me several times, but without avail, for the reason that I have already given. One evening, however, prayer was offered for me again. This time God gave the victory, rebuked the disease, and I was healed, although I was left very weak. The next evening prayer was again offered that my strength be restored, which petition God granted. The following morning Mother Bolds helped me to dress, and in company with her and Father Bolds and my brother, I got into a lumber-wagon and started to Joplin, Missouri, seven miles away, to begin a meeting.

That evening I testified, and the next day preached twice; although I could not walk alone, and had to be led by two persons for a week, and by one person for two weeks. It was two weeks before the saliva came into my mouth. During this time, also a number of disorders appeared on my body one after another, almost like new diseases. As each new affliction appeared, God helped me to trust him until it was removed.

All this time, however, God had enabled me to help in the services - to preach, to testify, or to pray - whatever seemed to be my duty. Although I seemed able to do so much in the services, yet my mental vigor seemed not to have been restored sufficiently for me to carry on a conversation; and between services, I would scarcely talk at all. Indeed, I was hardly able to think rationally very long at a time; but during the services when the anointing of God's Spirit was upon me, I hardly think any one could have told that I was laboring under any difficulties at all.

The meeting at Joplin lasted four weeks. During that time my brother got a call to another place, and I was left to finish the meeting alone. In many ways my body was not yet normal, but it was improving surprisingly fast. Soon after my brother left, Mother Bolds came to call on me, and I begged her to stay until the close of the series of meetings. I felt so helpless yet that I could not keep from crying like a child. She encouraged me as best she could, and told me that she would go home and see to things there, and then come back next day and stay with me until the meeting ended. She was a great encouragement to me and also a great help in the services.

Shortly after this I went with Father and Mother Bolds to help hold a meeting some distance from there in southern Missouri. Large crowds were in attendance, God blessed in the services, and souls were convicted and saved. A man and his wife who had professed to get saved, sent for us to come to their house, saying that they were sick. It was a peculiar case, one that we did not at all understand. Brother Bolds and I both went to God in earnest prayer, and the Lord revealed to each of us independently of the other that we had on hands a case of evil spirits. We laid on our hands, did all we could to cast them out; but as we did not know how to trust God for authority over them, they would not go.

While dealing with this case, I learned that the man and his father had a grudge against each other, and had not been on speaking terms for sometime. We remained at the house until the night service, when the brother started with us to meeting. We had to pass his father's house on the way. Before starting, the man had asked me privately whether or not he ought to get the difficulty out from between him and his father. I advised him that he should. So when we came to his father's house, he tried to ask his father's forgiveness; but instead of doing as he purposed, the devils began to talk through him and to make strange noises. The son's demonstrations stirred up the devil in his father, who began to rage against Brother Bolds, and to abuse him, calling him wicked vile names. I said to Sister Bolds: "The Lord has used us as well as Brother Bolds in the meeting, and I think we ought to be willing to take our share of the abuse. Let us go up where they are talking." As we appeared, the father turned on me. He said everything that the devil could bring to his mind, but the more he said, the happier I became. Finally, Brother Bolds said, "Sister Cole, I think we had better hurry on to meeting, as the congregation will be there and will be disappointed if we are late." It seemed that I could hardly tear myself away from the place, God was so wonderfully pouring his glory into my soul. The demon-possessed man came along with us, growling and whining like a dog, and making other strange noises. He kept up these demonstrations during the entire meeting. Some of the unsaved people seemed to understand just how matters were and enjoyed it immensely. They laughed and had great fun.

For two weeks afterward the devil-possessed man was completely deranged mentally. His father guarded the house and would not let Brother Bolds call on him; although, when the son saw Brother Bolds, he would say, "If you will let that man in, I will soon be all right." After two weeks his mental powers were restored, but he was completely turned against the truth, and would not come to meeting any more.

On the night of which we have been speaking, I had promised to go back and stay all night at the home of the son. During the night the Lord woke me up and brought to mind very forcibly that the powers of hell were there, and that I was in the presence of a murderous spirit. The Lord impressed me that I should lie awake and pray. Early in the morning my host began to call to me at the top of his voice: "Leave, old Satan! leave, old Satan!" My first thought was, "This is his home, and I shall be compelled to leave." Snow lay about a foot deep on the ground, and the air was cold and sharp. It was a mile to the nearest house. My next thought was, "Why, my name is not old Satan, and I will not answer to Satan's name; but if he calls me Mary Cole, and tells me to leave, I will go as soon as I can, because it is his place, and not mine."

He left the house and went to the barn to feed his stock. I got up and dressed and was impressed to remain until he came back, and then to ask him the privilege of having prayer with him. It seemed that he could not refuse my request. So I read and prayed. Up to this time, I had been bothered very much by my feelings; but now I just leaned on God alone, trusted in his word, claimed the promises, and prayed that he would bring me off more than conqueror. The Lord made me understand that he gave me power over all the powers of the enemy.

After prayer the man called me in to breakfast.

God had already shown me that he did not want me to eat breakfast; so I told the man I did not care for any. He insisted that I come, and began to cry; but I did not go. The door being open between the room where I was and the room in which they were eating, I heard him say, "Wife, I believe we are mistaken; I believe those are the people of God." The next morning being Sunday, he went with me to the meeting, but that was the last one he attended.

This was but a short time after I had the typhoid fever. The fight with the enemy in which I had been engaged, strengthened my faith greatly. I was now more ready to cope with devils than I had ever been before. I had been very weak on that point. Before the experience which I have just related, if I felt all right, I thought everything was all right; but if my feelings were not good, I began to doubt God's promises. God had just brought me off more than conqueror in a severe conflict, and I was now ready to take him at his word, no matter how the enemy raged, and no matter how bad I felt. My faith was now grounded in knowledge.

During the meeting we were then holding, we had to endure some persecutions. One cold night some one put red pepper on the stove. The stove was in the center of the room, and the fumes from the pepper almost stifled the people. They had to run out to keep from choking. Brother Bolds quickly raised the window opposite the door, and the draft between the window and the door soon drove the stifling fumes from the house. Although the people were so affected by the fumes of the pepper, yet we ministers did not suffer a bit. Twice during this meeting we were egged - once with frozen eggs. None of the eggs, however, hit any of us. Two persons who were not fully decided to stand for the truth, got some benefit of the eggs. On the road to meeting one night, some of the opposers of the truth were egged by their comrades, who mistook them for members of our company.

Several times after getting light on the church I had the privilege of helping in meetings in my own home. These were attended with good results: a few got deliverance and were established in the whole truth. Some are true to God yet. One time while at my home, Sister Lodema Kaser and I went to a little town named Greenridge, about ten miles away; and, being solicited by some good honest souls to hold a meeting, we began services at that place. A good interest soon began to be manifested: conviction settled on the people, and hands began to go up for prayer. The meetings had continued nearly a week, when we received a pressing call from Kansas to come at once to hold services in a certain town. As God was working in a marvelous way where we were, I did not feel clear to go. Even after prayer I still felt that we should continue the meeting where we were.

The second letter had come, I think, insisting that we should come. Then I began to infer that if I did not heed this call, they would think that I was refusing because I was so near home. So I submitted and went. To the surprise of the brother who had asked us to come, the Spirit of the Lord did not work in the meeting. The brother soon saw his mistake and asked my pardon. He said, "Sister Cole, I will never do such a thing again."

We did not remain long at this place. The only fruit of our labors, so far as we know, was one dear sister who got under conviction, but who did not get a chance to become acquainted with the whole truth until fifteen years afterward, but the light that she got at that time and the conviction that came upon her, followed her until she was gloriously saved. This was Sister Matilda Magley. The last news I had from her, she was a precious saint of God. Another result of this meeting was, that we learned a good lesson. In the future, we were more careful how we let others persuade us out of God's order.

I hold that God's true ministers who live close to him are able to get their own leadings from the Lord, especially where souls are at stake. God wants us to have our own individuality. True, the Word says, "Be subject to one another," but we are to be subject always in conformity with his will and his Word. I know that I have had to trust my individual leading; I have had to depend upon them to keep me from being led off by wrong influences and spirits. When I saw my privilege to individually learn God's will, I took advantage of it, and I have had reason to thank God for the protection of his Spirit.

God's children should be very careful not to urge his servants away from a place before God says go, nor should they urge them to come to a place until God is through with them where they are laboring. By so doing, souls may be lost that otherwise would be saved. At one time I had four pressing calls to hold meetings in different places, and every one of them contained the promise, "We will pay your fare both ways if you will come." God showed me that I should not accept any of them; but should go in another direction, taking my own money to pay my fare. I went, happy in knowing that I was in God's order. Dear ones, let us depend upon the leadings of God's Spirit, and not allow our financial interests to bias our decisions.

While traveling in the West, Brother Warner and his company had held a meeting at Galesburg, Kansas, in which a certain woman was saved. Previous to this time she had been a member of a sect and was unsaved. Her husband, who was a doctor and had once had an experience of salvation, was greatly delighted to think that his wife had an experimental knowledge of Christ. It seemed that he could scarcely have been happier had he been saved himself. After his wife was saved, he sent for Sister Kaser and me to come and hold a meeting. We came; but when he met us at the train, we were not the capable-looking people that he expected to see, and he was quite taken aback. Nevertheless, he invited us to his house and was very hospitable. We found his wife to be a precious saint.

The meetings began; conviction came upon the people; and God began to save souls. Our burden was mostly for the soul of the doctor. At first he seemed quite unconcerned about himself, but much concerned for others. But God was working, and conviction soon fastened upon him. At last I ventured to ask him to raise his hand for prayer, which he did. Next day I asked him to take further steps toward his salvation; but he said, "Sister Cole, I did as you asked me to last night, and I don't feel any better - I feel worse." I did what I could to encourage him, and the Spirit of the Lord continued to work with him. After meeting one night, his load had become so heavy he could not carry it any longer, and he then and there requested earnest prayer. It was near midnight before God spoke peace to his soul, but a happier person you could hardly find. He soon saw that the old sin principle was still in his heart and the enemy suggested, "Do not get sanctified; you will have to give up certain things that you won't care to give up yet. Just live a good justified life." In some way God gave him a warning that he must seek sanctification. He heeded God's voice, came to the altar, and was fully sanctified. God soon had his hand on him for the work. This was Bro. S. G. Bryant.

A man at Essex, Illinois, became interested in the meetings we were holding there. He was educated in four different languages, made a profession of religion, and belonged, I think, to some denomination, but had no experience of salvation. He soon saw that he needed help from God and came to the altar. He had a desperate struggle. He said his education did not help him to get saved, but was only a hindrance, and got between him and God. He wept and plead with God just like any other poor sinner, and finally broke loose from the things that seemed to hinder him and was made to rejoice in the Savior's love. Later he came to the altar and was sanctified. Soon God's hand was on him for spiritual work, and later he became a minister. This was Bro. Addison Kriebel.

This incident shows that while education is all right and a good thing to have, yet it is no help in seeking the Lord. The scripture says, that the wisdom of this world is foolishness with God. Nor will education bring soul-rest; it can not be substituted for spirituality. Education, however, need not be a hindrance to spirituality if spirituality be made the master and education the servant. If this relationship be maintained, the child of God is safe in the possession of education.

At one time my brother Jeremiah was talking to a professor of a college about his soul, and trying to get him to seek the Lord. The professor seemed to be full of learning, and his affections were so set on the things of this world, that Jeremiah could scarcely make any impression on him. While they were talking, the professor's little two-year-old child, who was playing near by, came up and said, "Papa, Papa, put your affections on things above," and returned again to her play. "There," said my brother, "can you take that? Can you accept the lesson the Lord wants to give you?" Wise as the professor was, he was confounded, knowing that God must have put this speech into the heart of his little child to reprove him. "Out of the mouth of babes and sucklings hast thou ordained strength, because of thine enemies, that thou mightest still the enemy and the avenger" (Psalm 8:2).

At one time when Sister Kaser had been called home, I went home on a visit. While there, I got a call to Meridian, Kansas, to hold a meeting. I arrived at the town on an early morning train, remained in the depot until daylight, and then hired a boy to carry my valise to the home of the minister, Mr. J. W. Wyrick, who was pastor at that place. The door was opened in response to my knock; and, as I stepped in, I received a very strange impression.

The disordered house struck me peculiarly; but my

mind was relieved when the man said that his child was lying very sick and that they had been taking turns sitting up with it. In an inner room, I found his wife, a pitiful, sad-looking person, with a face that bespoke trouble. I kept my feelings and thoughts to myself, knowing that the Lord was able to guide me aright and to use me to his glory. I felt wonderfully impressed, however, with the presence of evil spirits. Not being able to locate them, or to reach any definite conclusion, I waited for further developments.

The meeting began. There were at least three factions in the congregation, and I could see but very little good in any of them. The man at whose house I was staying, claimed to represent the church of God. Meeting had continued but a little while before his conduct showed me his spiritual condition, and God wonderfully burdened me for his soul. While he was in prayer, God showed me that his case was serious, and that he was badly under the power of the enemy. It happened at the meeting. The young folks were misbehaving during prayer-time, and Mr. Wyrick prayed against them so vindictively that it was not hard to tell of what spirit he was.

I soon felt led to renounce the wrong spirit that Mr. Wyrick had already exhibited in prayer. This stirred him up. He knew that he had not been acting right, and he insisted that I should come to his home for a talk. I did not feel led to go to his house; but he insisted from time to time. Finally his wife came to me and said, "I wish you would come to the house, as it might make my husband treat me better." For her sake I went; but oh, the awful spirit I met!

If there had been any want of evidence as to the man's

condition, that want was now supplied. He began a tirade - said that Eve was the downfall of the world, and number of other things derogatory to woman's character. He told me that he had had a dream in which a forked-tongued snake had been trying to kill him. "You," said he, "are that forked-tongued snake." I told him that I could bear his abuse for Christ's sake. "But it is not for Christ's sake; it is your own devilish work." I could not reason with him at all, and so I said, "Let us pray." First I prayed, and then he prayed - an abusive prayer against me. He kept pouring out his abusive talk, until I closed the door - "slammed it," he said, which was false. God kept me clear through it all; but he made me to know that he did not want me to meet such cases alone any more, that others should be present to be agreed with me, and to stand against the powers of hell.

For several years my youngest brother, George, had been impressed that God wanted him to go into gospel work. He came to where we were then holding meeting. He seemed to think that God had sent him to us for the especial purpose of making me more useful and effectual in gospel work, which no doubt was the case. Nevertheless, God had a deeper design in his coming.

We were soon to go East to a camp-meeting. Although, when George left home he had only means enough to take him to the camp-meeting, yet God had shown him that he should come farther west before he went to the meeting. Before the time came for us to start, the railroad had cut rates so that we could travel for about one-third fare. God had worked it out so that we all could attend the meeting.

At a meeting Brother George and I were holding in Illinois, there was a brother who wanted to walk by faith. He thought that in order to make a success of such an experience he would have to ask the Lord to take away all feeling. I suppose he must have prayed until he got his prayer through, for God certainly did withdraw all good feelings from him. He took a severe affliction which caused his face and parts of his body to swell badly, and which brought on intense suffering. God seemed to be present when we prayed for him, but the brother was not healed, and his suffering became so severe that we were greatly burdened for him, and went to God in very earnest prayer to know wherein the difficulty lay. God showed us how the brother had prayed, and when we told him what the Lord had revealed to us, he saw his mistake and made matters right with the Lord, then he was soon gloriously healed. I have no idea that he ever asked the Lord again to take away all good feelings so as to enjoy walking by faith.

Some few years later, while Sister Kaser, my brother and I were in Robinson, Kansas, at a camp-meeting word came that my father was very sick and wished my brother and me to come at once. Brother Warner and his company were in this meeting. God was gloriously working, and souls were being saved. When the letter came, therefore, we felt very reluctant to leave, and after going to God in earnest prayer, we could not feel that he wanted us to start that day. Besides, I felt impressed that if we should start that day we should not get through to see him alive anyway, so we delayed our trip until the day following.

For about two weeks God had been impressing me that I was going to have a severe trial, at the same time bringing to me these comforting words: "I will go with you through it." This promise had been on my mind many times. The next morning we got a telegram that father was dead, and the enemy tried to crush me with the accusation that I did not love my father or I would have started to him the day before. Upon receipt of this telegram George and I started at once. We had not proceeded far on our journey until we learned that the train we should have taken had we gone the day before, was wrecked. Some of the cars went into the river. The Lord's warning had possibly saved us from death; but if not, from unnecessary delay, because had we taken that train, we should not have reached our destination any sooner than we did.

As I stood and gazed upon the still form of my father and remembered that a great deal of his Christian life had not been satisfactory, I wished I could have talked with him before he was taken.

The night after the funeral, when I had retired to rest, God began to talk to me. "Did I not tell you that you were going to pass through deep waters?" "Yes." "Did I not tell you that I would go through with you?" "Yes." "Have I not done as I promised?" "Yes." Certainly he was a present help - all and more than I could have wished - yes, and more than I comprehended at that time. I was so sustained that I did not at all realize the weight of the burden, because Jesus bore it for me.

A little later God seemed to withdraw some of his sustaining power and let me feel to some degree how heavy the burden really was. It seemed that the life would be crushed out of me. I asked the Lord the reason, and he plainly showed me that if he had not withdrawn his sustaining power I should never have known what a burden he had been bearing for me. I thought, too, that another object, no doubt, was to develop in me greater sympathy for others carrying a similar load.

As I still felt burdened for the salvation of souls at Robinson, Kansas, I returned to that place, and my brother remained to look after father's business. God gave me stirring messages. A number of souls that had been convicted got down to business and were saved. God's design was accomplished, and my soul was relieved.

Our next place of meeting was Wichita, Kans. Our company was to join Brother Warner's company in a camp-meeting at that place. He had received the money to defray the traveling-expenses of both companies. Our company was to meet them at the Robinson depot on a certain morning, and all were to travel together. There had been some misunderstanding, so Sister Kaser and I were not present. Brother Warner, therefore, left word that we should borrow the money and that he would make it right with us when we reached our destination.

Sister Kaser and I did not start until the following morning. We told the saints about the misunderstanding and explained that we did not have the money to pay our way. They did not make us a loan, but gave us the money. Not knowing how much the fare was, we asked for too small a sum, not wishing to ask for any more than we absolutely needed.

We could buy a ticket only to St. Joseph, Missouri, our first stopping-place, and therefore we did not know how much money we lacked, until we reached that place and asked for tickets to Wichita. To our surprise, we found that we had just enough to pay our way to Newton, Kansas, twenty miles east of Wichita. At first we felt somewhat dismayed to think of going without money to a strange town. We told the station agent of our predicament and also of our having friends at both ends of the road, and asked him what we had better do. He advised us to send a telegram to both places. In the meanwhile we sent a telegram up to the Lord, and he showed us that we should buy our tickets to Newton and trust him to bring matters out all right. We were shouting, happy. I remarked to Sister Kaser, "If some of these people on the train knew our circumstances and knew how happy we are, they would think we were ready for the insane asylum."

In the meantime, my brother George was planning to attend the same camp-meeting. He did not know what day we were going, nor did we know the day he was going. After he got started, he found that he was on a road that made very poor connections, and said to himself, "If I did not know that God was leading me to go this way, I should surely think I was out of order." Just before we got to Newton, where we thought we should have to stop because we had no money to go further, George got on the train, rode with us to Newton, got off at the station, and bought our tickets on to Wichita, and we did not have to leave our seats.

When we got to the meeting, Brother Warner helped us to take a good shout, and refunded the money that had been given him to pay our fares. We had a glorious camp-meeting and numbers were saved. Hypocrites made some disturbance, but God overruled.

While here we met a man by the name of Joseph Prouse, who invited us to come to his place to hold a meeting. We went. The meeting had been in progress three days, when, as we were in a private conversation, talking about the nationality of those present, we found out that Brother Prouse was related to my family. His mother and my mother were half-sisters, both being children of the same father. Brother Prouse was the first relative of ours that we had ever met or heard of that had accepted the whole truth. Not only Brother Prouse was saved, but also his wife and some of his children. Truly we had a time of great rejoicing. It seemed so good to find some of our relatives that knew God and were living Christian lives. The event was so unexpected and such a glad surprise that we praised the Lord together.

Shortly before going to Galesburg, Kansas, to hold a meeting, I received a few lines from Brother Warner telling me that two gospel workers, a man and a woman, would join me at that place. In his letter he gave me to understand their spiritual condition so that we should know how to proceed for their good and our own protection. The brother at the place where we were holding the meeting had been saved but a very short time, and was not therefore able to discern false spirits. When he saw that there was no fellowship between these two people and our company, he was tempted to think that it was because we did not have compassion for them. God soon showed him, however, that they were in a bad spiritual condition and that our company was all right. From that time we had his help and encouragement.

After a day of prayer and fasting for the couple that needed help, they both humbled themselves. The man fell to the floor stiff under the power of the enemy, but the woman desired deliverance. So far as we could understand, God delivered both of them, but as they did not take a stand against the evil spirits that had been troubling them, they got into the same condition again. Under the influence of a spirit of accusation, they wrote a letter to Brother Warner finding fault with our company of workers.

Bro. Charlie Williams, who was at that time a member of our company, was corresponding with Brother Warner. In his letters Brother Warner would say, "God bless you, Brother Charlie!" but he would never say, "God bless you. Sister Kaser and Sister Cole!" At that time the enemy was coming against our souls with terrible accusing power, and we felt that we needed a blessing very much. The accusations of the enemy continued for about two weeks, during which time it seemed that our lives would be crushed out of us. Waking up early one morning, I said, "O Lord! why is it I can't get consolation from a certain source," meaning "Why can't I get an encouraging letter from Brother Warner!" The Lord answered, "I will give you consolation first-handed if you will accept it." My heart opened up to God as a little flower opens to the morning dew, and oh, how I drank in the good things of the kingdom!

Then as I found myself, as it were, in a large room with the Lord, feasting on his beauties, his grandeur and glory, the scripture came so forcibly to me: "A day in thy courts is better than a thousand. I would rather be a doorkeeper in the house of my God, than to dwell in the tents of wickedness" (Psalm 84:10). In my thought I could compare my experience to that of a little child accustomed to but few pretty things and poor surroundings who was put into a beautiful parlor containing all sorts of beautiful things for its pleasure. Being told to help itself, it would walk up and down the room with delight, hardly knowing what to take hold of or to enjoy first. In this experience through which I had just passed, I learned the precious lesson that trial is to God's true children like a wine-press to the grape. As the wine-press brings out the pure juice of the grape, so the trials of a child of God bring out and puts on exhibition a pure Christian character.

On going East soon after these events, we met Brother Warner and told him of our experience and of Satan's tempting us to think that he would renounce us. He answered: "No, Sister Cole, we we wouldn't have renounced you, but had we been near enough and had known what you were passing through, we would, had it been in our power, have gone to you and done all we could to help you."

During the first summer that my youngest brother was with us in the work, he did not take a very active part. There were several reasons for this. Before leaving home he was nearly broken down through overwork. Besides, like almost all young workers, he was timid and backward, and needed encouragement and support. When the battle was strong, he would not be able to bear much responsibility. I would doubtless have been tempted in regard to my brother's condition had not God made me to know that I must be patient and give his body time to recuperate and give him a chance to develop as a worker.

Late in the fall we began a series of meetings in company with another gospel worker who had been in the work for sometime. This worker suggested to me in the early part of the meeting, "You and I will do the preaching, and toward the end your brother can have an opportunity to exercise himself." He spoke as though, should my brother try to take part, the meeting would be spoiled. I said but little in reply, feeling sure that God was able to manage things. As a result of this brother's attitude, however, the accuser also turned on my brother's soul, and as a result, discouragements set in on him thick and fast. I felt that something was going wrong and spoke about it to the older brother, telling him that George needed encouragement and not holding back, as he was timid. The brother assured me that he was giving George all the encouragement he could.

Not long after the events of which I have been speaking, I had a dream in which I thought my brother told me that this minister was holding him back and at the same time whipping him and finding fault with him for not moving out. When I awoke, I told the dream to a sister with the remark, "Well, this is nothing but a dream, and I don't believe there is anything in it." Nevertheless, it troubled my mind until I asked my brother about the matter, concluding with the remark, "I guess there isn't anything in it." He answered, "Yes, Mary, I guess there is something in it," and began to cry. God stirred up my soul, and at the first opportunity I talked to the older brother and told him what God had shown me in a dream. He said, "Oh, your brother has been talking to you about it." I said.

"No, God showed me first, and then I asked my brother about it." The brother promised that he would never do so again.

George and I visited a brother (Harvey W.) of ours that

we had not seen for nineteen years, not since I was a little girl and sorely afflicted. He looked at me with big tears running down his cheeks and said, "Mary, I can see that God has done more for you than you can understand, as I have not seen you for so long." A few months later, upon his invitation we came and held a series of meetings in his neighborhood. He had once been a Protestant Methodist preacher, and had enjoyed an experience of salvation, but had been quite doctrinized in the "one-work theory." When we came to hold a meeting, he began to defend his pet theory. I soon saw there was no use to explain the Scriptures to him, as he was unsaved, so I said to him: "Now, Harvey, you know you haven't got the first work, so we will not argue about the second. Come to the Lord. Let him forgive you and save you from your sins, and if you find that you get sanctified at the same time, we will gladly accept your doctrine, but if not, you will know it." Before the meeting closed, he came to the altar, called on God for mercy, and obtained forgiveness. As he arose from the altar, I came to him, praised die Lord with him and said, "Now, brother, do you know that you have received both justification and sanctification?" "No, Mary," he said, "I think I did well to get my sins forgiven."

We were once holding a camp-meeting in Nebraska at a new place. The Spirit of the Lord was working mightily. Souls were being saved and sanctified, and bodies were being healed. Much was to be done, and especially toward the close of the meeting our time was fully occupied. While we were the busiest, a brother brought an insane woman to the camp-meeting for healing. Her husband accompanied her. As we were so rushed with the general duties of the meeting, we had no time to give attention to so important a case until the meeting was over. We told the brother that if the man and his wife would remain until after the meeting was over, we would then do all we could for her deliverance.

The meeting closed on Sunday evening, and on Monday afternoon after we had packed our things ready for the next meeting, we took the case under consideration and sought the Lord for wisdom as to what should be done, and one of the company (George) obtained this promise: "God does not give us the spirit of fear, but of love, of power, and of a sound mind." While we were at prayer, the insane woman was down-stairs with a little girl, to whom she remarked, "My prayers are up-stairs." She seemed in some way to be conscious that something was being done for her benefit.

The woman for whom we had been praying had before her marriage been a bright, intelligent teacher.

Before she became afflicted, she weighed 190 pounds, but at the time of which we are speaking, she weighed only 110 pounds. I can not say positively what was the cause of her insanity; but as near as I remember, she wished to become a Christian, and as some of her relatives opposed, her mind gradually became unbalanced. At the time she came to us for prayer, they said she did not sleep for a whole hour during any night, but was walking, talking, or moving about in some way.

As we waited on the Lord in her behalf, our souls were encouraged. We came down-stairs, anointed the woman, prayed for her, and claimed the promises; but when we arose from our knees, she was, so far as we could see, ten times worse than before. We did not look at outward appearances, however, but praised God and rested on his promises and counted him faithful in fulfilling them.

That evening we went our different ways, but before we separated, we could see a marked change in her for the better. My brother asked them to keep us posted as to how she got along, and about a week later we received word that she was much better and was improving rapidly. About six weeks afterward, I think it was, they said there was scarcely any signs of her insanity. She had resumed her duties as mother and housewife, and was gaining flesh. Just a short time before this latter report, it was said that upon the appearance of some little symptom of her former malady, one of her relatives tried to make her take medicine. The brother who related the story, said in his peculiar German way, that she "spitted it out and wouldn't take it." So far as we have ever learned, the sister was fully restored to health.

When we are earnestly looking to God in behalf of some one who needs help, and he gives us a precious promise, it is undoubtedly our privilege and duty to claim the promise and to be strengthened and encouraged thereby. If God does not want to work in the case, doubtless he will not impress us with a promise in this way. At such times we should not feel timid. God is leading, and if we will move forward in faith as rapidly as he leads us, he is sure to bring us off more than conqueror.

While working in Oklahoma, we became acquainted with the members of a new sect known as "The Followers." Some articles of their faith were similar to those of the Christian, or Cambellite, denomination. Besides these, they believed in the reception of the Holy Ghost by the laying on of hands; they professed to speak in tongues and to interpret, a demonstration which God made us to know was a deception of the devil. But the most peculiar tenet of their faith was that their members were not counted perfect until they could pick up a snake without injury. This belief was, we suppose, based on the scripture found in Mark 16:18: "They shall take up serpents." A number of them were able to do this without any bad result, but a few were bitten so badly that they came near dying. The Lord made us to understand so clearly the spiritual condition of these people that we felt clear in pointing out their delusion.

In a dream that I had at this time, I saw a ferocious wild animal coming to take my life. It seemed that if I could get hold of its horns God would protect me and help me to overcome it. During the meeting of which I have been speaking, we went home with one of the families of The Followers. As we were returning to the meeting in the evening, one of their number who professed to talk with tongues and to have great authority, began talking his jargon as though he were pronouncing vengeance on us. God gave me to understand that this was the wild animal of my dream and that I should trust God and rebuke the devil, which I did. God put his rebuke on the spirit, and that night, through us, exposed the false doctrine. One of the leaders came out, got a good experience of salvation, and became a minister of the present truth. A number of others also got established in the church of God.

Shortly after the events related above, we went to Nishnabotna, where we met a spirit similar to the one we had encountered at St. James, Mo. The demonstrations, however, were not quite so vile, but the spirit was making progress in the community and had a number under its influence. In their meetings they would jump and dance and talk about the great power they had. They declared it was God's power and that if any one went against it, something dreadful would happen to him. They even went so far as to say that if any one spoke against the demonstration they made or "the power," as they called it, God would strike him dead.

That same evening one of their number invited us to go home with him. Our conveyance was an old-fashioned farm-wagon. For some reason I did not feel clear in going alone, as the powers of the enemy were so plainly manifested. I therefore asked a certain sister to go with me. We had not gone far until the enemy came at me with great force. "Now you know what was said tonight-that those who opposed the power would be struck dead, and I am going to kill you." I said, "No, you are not." "Yes, I will." "No, you are not." I immediately leaned on God and trusted him for protection. Within a few minutes the enemy tried to carry his threat into effect. The wagon was on the side of a ridge about half way between the summit and the base of a high hill. On our left hand below us a number of feet lay a stream, on our right was a high cliff, and ahead of us was a team which began to balk and push back toward our wagon. For a few minutes it seemed that we must be either crushed by the big team in front or thrown into the stream, God came to our rescue, and the other team was brought under control before ours became very much excited. While the danger threatened us, however, we got out of the wagon, and the sister who was with me sprained her ankle badly. None of the rest of us were hurt. Again the Lord's promises were proved true and the devil a liar.

A number of people who had been under the false spirit, when they heard the truth and learned the difference between the workings of the Spirit of the Lord and the demonstrations of false, deceptive spirits, proved themselves honest at heart, took a stand against the enemy, and got deliverance. A number of them are still walking in the light of divine truth.

At the Beaver Dam, Indiana, camp-meeting I had rather an amusing experience. There was a woman on the grounds who had been delivered of evil spirits; but as she had not taken the proper stand against the enemy, she had again become possessed. I met her soon after my arrival, and she began almost immediately to try to teach me in regard to dress. As I understood her condition, I said to her plainly, "I know that you are devil-possessed. Wait until you get deliverance again, and then if God gives you a message I will receive it. I will not receive a message from the devil." She smiled and walked away.

A number of the sisters slept in an attic. As we were about to retire one night, the devil-possessed woman was acting like an insane person, throwing the bed-clothes down-stairs and acting in a way that showed that the devil had full control of her. Some of the sisters, becoming frightened, huddled in the corner of the room for fear she would hurt them. In the confusion, I forgot for the moment to trust in God. Instead of thinking of God and his protecting power, I thought that the enemy might touch the woman's brain, make her insane, and cause her to do almost any desperate deed. I thought it would be well to protect myself and acted accordingly. Just then Mother Smith, who had been informed of what was going on in the attic, came on the scene, and found the woman raging in the middle of the room and the rest of us huddled in the corners.

Mother Smith took in the situation at a glance, and, pointing a finger at me said: "Shame on you, Sister Mary! afraid of the devil! This is nothing but the work of the devil, and here you are hiding from the devil. Shame on you, Sister Mary!" It would be impossible to tell you how I felt, and so I shall not try, neither shall I make excuses nor plead my case. I came out of my corner and Mother Smith began at once to tell us what must be done. She said that the devil-possessed woman must sleep between her and me that night. She had her way. It was not a pleasant night, and I got but little rest. Every little while the woman would take a spell of choking and then laugh in a silly way. At such times Mother Smith and I would lay on our hands and rebuke the devil. We did this, not once, but many times. By morning I had learned my lesson and never from that day to this have I run from the devil.

When a soul wants to get deliverance, it is the duty and privilege of the minister to exercise heavenly authority. God has delegated to his New Testament ministry all the power that they need for every emergency. I heard of a minister, a sister, who, when evil spirits were to be cast out, became so frightened that she ran and climbed up on the woodpile. The brethren that were present, were greatly amused and asked her if the enemy had her treed. We need never fear the enemy nor give way to him in the least. If we keep our faith in the Master's promise, "behold, I give unto you.... power over all the power of the enemy: and nothing shall by any means hurt you." "Greater is he that is in you than he that is in the world." Let us remember always that in our own strength we can not expel evil spirits, but that all our power and authority in such cases come from God. If we keep our faith steadfast, the enemy can no more overcome us than he can overcome God himself.

Mary Cole

Chapter XV

Various Experiences - Continued

Sometime after I got light on the one body, I was helping Brothers Kilpatrick and Speck in a camp-meeting near Essex, Ill. For three days I was under a severe trial or burden, which became heavier and heavier until it was unbearable. The worst of my difficulty was that I did not know what was the matter.

Finally I went to my room, locked the door, threw myself on the bed and cried, "Lord, you must show me what is the matter; I can't stand this any longer." Then the Lord began to talk to me in a loving, fatherly, encouraging way: "This is a battle between God and the devil. Are you willing to fight in it?" "Yes, Lord," I said, "with all my heart"; and almost before I could think, the cloud was all gone, the burden had disappeared, and I was as happy and triumphant as I had ever been. I don't think I had another test during that meeting.

Through this peculiar experience I learned the difference between soul-burden and condemnation and between accusation and conviction, as I had never been able to comprehend it before, although I thought I had understood this difference measurably well. Many dear souls have been troubled on these subjects, mistaking soul-burden for condemnation and accusation for conviction. A clear understanding of the difference between these soul experiences will save us from many unnecessary trials. I have been thankful ever since for God's teaching.

While in evangelistic work I had the privilege of attending meetings of various kinds in many different States. Shortly before the Gospel Trumpet office was moved to Moundsville, our company attended a camp-meeting at that place. Brother Clayton's earnest labors were beginning to show some results, but the work was still quite new. We arrived there the afternoon before the general meeting began. But little preparation had been made to accommodate the workers who would be present. My brother George had found a place to stay, but nothing had been said to me about lodging. Just before the beginning of the services, a woman came to me and asked if I would go home with her. I did not feel favorably impressed, and thought I would wait and see if I should get another invitation. The night services closed, and no one had yet offered me lodging, so I accepted the woman's invitation. I had been kept awake two nights on my trip to the meeting, and now I had to walk a mile before retiring. As we drew near the house, I felt the awful powers of the enemy coming against my soul. I wondered what kind of place I was going to, but it was too late to turn back. Although it was ten o'clock at night, we met the woman's little grandchild out playing, and the child was by no means in an inviting condition.

When we reached the house I understood at once why I had not felt impressed to accept the woman's invitation. Everything was in disorder, and the house was almost as filthy as a swine-pen. The floor was covered with sand on which tobacco-juice was freely sprinkled, and over this filth the beds had been laid down. The woman had already told me that she had a nice clean bed for me in an upstairs room, and in this I hoped to find the rest I so much needed. After eating, with considerable difficulty, a little lunch set before me, I was shown to my room, which had a more cleanly appearance than the room down-stairs. I wanted very much to lock my door; but as I could not, committed myself to God's care, and went to bed.

Vermin of different kinds prevented sleep; and not long after going to bed I heard a noise downstairs that indicated the arrival of company of no desirable sort. My heart began to sink within me. "O Lord!" said I, "why have you let me come to a place like this?" and the tears began to course down my cheeks. The answer came, "That you may have an opportunity to be partaker of my suffering." I thought to myself, "I am a poor specimen to fulfil that scripture tonight." I do not believe I slept ten minutes the whole night through. I heard the town-clock every time it struck; but during that night of anxiety and prayer I learned the lesson that I must be ready at all times and under all circumstance, to partake of Christ's suffering, and that in order to partake of his sufferings, I must be very little and very humble. Next morning, with veiled face, I made my way to the camp-ground in as round-a-bout way as I could, so that no one would know where I lodged the night before, and thus reproach be brought upon the cause of Christ.

Our next camp-meeting was at Mole Hill, W. Virginia. This was a new place, and not many attended the services; but the Lord blessed in the presentation of the Word, and we had a good meeting. It closed on

Sunday. Just before the services on Saturday night, an armed mob came into the camp. Never in all my life had I heard so many awful oaths in so short a time. A number of unsaved young men who lived in that neighborhood and who were favorable to the truth, undertook to defend us and to keep the meeting from being broken up. The mob said that they had come on purpose to tear the tent down, but those who were defending us said that they should not, and that if they undertook to carry out their threat they would be "laid low," meaning that they would kill them. A number of shots were exchanged between the two parties, some of which came very close to me. You may think it very foolish, but I found myself dodging behind the canvas for protection. Afterwards I was amused at myself, but at such a time the weakness of humanity is on exhibition.

After the two parties had continued for nearly an hour, I think, I felt strongly impressed that a number of us should kneel down and call earnestly on God for protection. While we were on our knees, God made me to know that none of us should be hurt and that the tabernacle should not suffer damage. I arose from my knees with victory. Not long afterward the young men who were protecting us, got our assailants on the run. They left in such a hurry that one of their number left his hat behind. He made several attempts to come back after it, but our boys always headed him off. The strife lasted all night, and no one in the camp got any rest. At midnight a sister who for a long time had been seeking sanctification, but had not been able to get the experience, came to the Lord, made the consecration, was made happy, and began singing:

"Hallelujah for the cleansing!

It has reached my inmost soul,
For the glory now is streaming;
Praise the Lord, He makes me whole!"

The next day was a very busy day. God worked mightily. Souls were saved and sanctified, and bodies were healed. It was a day of victory from beginning to end. I had asked the Lord not to let "a dog move his tongue" against the tent. Nothing about the camp was disturbed.

Several times during my ministry the Lord has laid upon my heart a message to deliver, and has not made my burden known to the other ministers present. As such times, if one is not very true and faithful to God, he is likely to be accused of the enemy and so prevented from doing his duty. The first experience of this kind that I remember, occurred at a camp-meeting in the State of Indiana. One Sunday when a very large crowd was in attendance, a sectarian minister who seemed to be getting out of Babylon was expected to preach. The brethren thought it would encourage him and edify the congregation. In the afternoon I overheard some of the ministers encouraging him to deliver a message. God made me to understand that this man was not making the progress that he should and that he was not in a condition to deliver a message, especially at such a time. I was looking very earnestly to the Lord when he made me to know that he wanted me to deliver the message, but I knew from what I had heard that he had not made it known to the other ministers.

This state of affairs put me in a very trying place; for if I should take the pulpit, it would look as if I wanted to be too forward, thus hindering one who might have the message. The conviction on my heart was so great, however, and God's hand so heavy upon me for this duty, that I got up; but as I was stepping into the pulpit, I saw the sectarian minister with his Bible in his hand just ready to rise to his feet. "Oh, pardon me," said I. "No, you pardon me; go ahead," he replied. "No, you go ahead." "Oh, my message won't spoil." "Mine won't either," I replied. Then he again insisted upon my going ahead; and as I knew God was ordering it, I delivered the message and God wonderfully blessed my soul.

Not until the evening service did the other ministers realize that God was putting me forward to deliver the message. That night when there were not more than one-third as many present as there were in the afternoon, the minister of whom I have been speaking, rose to preach. His sermon was nothing but a message from the devil. God's ministers were disgusted. Mother Sarah Smith, who sat right in front of the pulpit and who always encouraged the ministers and held up their hands with her "Amen! Praise the Lord!" began in her usual way. I said to myself, "If I have not misunderstood the voice of God, her amens will stop and her head will go down before this message is ended." It was not long until her amens ceased. Before the sermon was ended, some of the ministers were pacing the grounds in agony because the enemy was filling the pulpit, and some of the sinners felt like taking the ministers out and giving them a threshing because they had permitted such a thing.

It was over at last. Brother Warner came to me and said: "Sister Cole, I can see now why God had you take the pulpit in the afternoon when the largest crowd was present. There would have been much more harm done, had he preached then instead of tonight." This experience emphasized to me the fact that it pays to obey God. First, be sure that God is ordering your steps, and then be true to God. He will stand by you though you have to go through fire to do his bidding.

At a camp-meeting in Michigan God made it clear to my soul that at the evening service he wanted me to deliver a message especially for the benefit of backsliders. The burden upon me was so great that I could hardly sit still until time for preaching. In the prayer just before the sermon, the brother who led made it very clear that he was sure God was going to have him deliver the message that night. I sympathized with him, of course, and did not want him to have any unnecessary trial; neither did I want to disobey God.

I submitted the matter to the Lord, telling him that if he still wanted me to deliver the message, to hold the brother back until it would not appear that I was trying to get ahead of him. God wonderfully owned and blessed his Word, and a number of backsliders were reclaimed. After the service, the brother who had thought he had the message came to me and said, "Sister Cole, I did think I had the message, but the Lord blessed you." "Yes," I said, "the Lord blessed me in obeying; but it took more grace than usual."

At a Kansas camp-meeting there was a man present who had not been living a consistent Christian life. He had done things that disqualified him for preaching. I told the Lord that I would do anything he showed me in order to keep the pulpit clean.

As is usual at such gatherings, the largest crowd was present on Sunday afternoon. I saw the minister of whom I had just spoken, getting ready to take the pulpit. It came to my mind that if I wanted to obey the Lord and to keep my promise I must act quickly. I asked the Lord to exercise his control and to give me the needed opportunity to obey. He did, and I preached the sermon that day. Very soon afterward an accident occurred in which this minister's false teeth were broken, so that he could not preach during the remainder of the meeting. Thus God's cause was protected.

To obey the Lord under the circumstances of which I have just been speaking, takes much grace, especially on the part of the minister who knows the proper attitude toward his fellow ministers and desires to show them courtesy. At different times when I have felt led to move out and deliver a message, others have got ahead of me so that I did not have an opportunity at that time. Frequently under such circumstances God has opened the way for me to deliver the message later and has made it more effectual than it would have been had I delivered it when I first desired to do so. Now, I would not advise workers or ministers to make unusual efforts to get into the pulpit, unless they knew beyond a doubt that God is ordering. But if you are certain of the leadings of the Lord, even if God does not make it plain to others, you may do as God bids you with certainty of success.

In a certain meeting I had the message, but another minister took the pulpit so quickly that I had no chance to deliver it. At the close of the service, a number of persons came to me saying, "Sister Cole, you had the message." "Yes," I answered, "I felt sure I did, but I had no chance to deliver it." "Well, maybe God will give you a chance to deliver it yet." "I think he will if he wants it delivered," I replied, "and perhaps when I do have an opportunity, the message will be stronger - boiled down, as it were." The opportunity came the following day. At that time there were present in the meeting a minister and some of his congregation who had gotten out of the way. God so blessed the delivery of the Word that not only the minister but also a number from his congregation got delivered.

Isaiah's prophecy that the blind eyes should be opened, was fulfilled during the time of Jesus' earthly ministry, and it is being fulfilled today. I have been a witness to a number of such healings, of which I will relate three.

While my brother George and I were holding a meeting in Nebraska, a lady, accompanied by her husband, came a number of miles to be healed of blindness. She was not a saint, nor do I think that she had even been professing. Be that as it may, she had heard that the Lord was healing people. She was so nearly blind that she could not see to sew or read, and could scarcely do her housework at all. At first we talked to her about her soul, and she expressed a desire to get right with God. When asked whether she would rather have salvation or healing, she chose salvation first. We all bowed before the Lord, and asked him to save her soul. She got the witness that she was saved. Although we did not make her healing a special subject of prayer, yet we asked God to do for her eyes all that he saw fit.

The following day she went home, and not long afterward we heard that she was much better. After another brief interval of time we heard that her eyes were well and that she could read and sew just as she did before they became afflicted. Her friends who brought her to the meeting for healing were very much tried when we instructed her to seek salvation before healing. They thought that she would be discouraged because we did not make a specialty of her healing. After all, it turned out all right, thus showing that God's way is best.

A brother, an old man, came to an Oklahoma camp-meeting for prayer. He had been a sinner from child-hood, and at the time of which I write, had been saved but little more than a year. A number of us anointed him and asked God to heal him of rheumatism and of everything else that he saw fit. One of the brother's eyes was in such bad condition that with it he could not distinguish a person from other objects. Soon after prayer was offered, he said the diseased eye had been fully restored.

One of the workers in the Chicago Home began to go blind in one of her eyes. The sight kept failing until it was entirely lost. We had prayer, claimed the healing on the authority of God's Word, and did not doubt, although the sight was not restored immediately. For two months she could tell but very little difference in the condition of her eye; but during this time, she held steadily on to God's promise and did not doubt him. At last God saw fit to give her the desire of her heart. Her faith was realized and her sight was restored.

Chapter XVI

God's Care Over Me

A number of times during my life I have been exposed to danger, but have always realized God's protecting hand. The incidents which I shall now relate, show God's goodness and tender care for me. Truly he is a present help in every time of need, and powerful to deliver under all circumstances.

One time while I was still in the old home at Windsor, Missouri, I was alone in the house. My parents had gone on a visit about twenty miles away, and two of my younger brothers were somewhere about the farm. I was in the room before the old-fashioned fireplace. Some embers had dropped out on the hearth, and ashes had settled over them, entirely hiding them from view. Presently I knelt on the hearth before the fire and began earnestly calling on God, my calico dress resting on the covered embers on the hearth. Being entirely absorbed in my devotion, I did not know that there was any danger until the flames were going up my back. I rushed to the door, calling loudly for help, in the hope that some one would hear me and come to my assistance. My next thought was to run to the kitchen, get some water, and throw it on the fire; but the thought flashed through my mind that if I should run through the hall, the fire would get such a headway that it would burn me to death. So I called on God earnestly: "O Lord, why is it that I am left here to burn to death alone?" With all my soul, I threw myself on his mercy. Like a good, loving, heavenly Father, he brought it to my mind to go to the closed door and press my back tightly against it until the flames were smothered. Although my clothes were nearly burned from my back, yet I escaped without the slightest injury. Truly God proved himself to be my wisdom and my deliverer.

While we were attending a meeting at Sturgeon, Missouri, I was a guest at a farm-house two or three miles from the town. I had no way of returning to town the next day, except to ride in on horseback. Because of my illness in early life, I had never learned to ride on horseback. My parents would never let me try, for fear that I should have a fit, fall from the horse, and be killed. At the place where I was staying, only two horses could be spared from the work on the farm - one gentle animal, too old to work on the farm, the other a fractious colt not sufficiently broken to be safe for a woman to ride. In fact, the young horse had thrown the young woman of the household a number of times.

There were three of us to go to town on these two horses - two other young women and I. The old lady had asked me if I was used to riding, and upon hearing that I was not, she said I should ride the old horse. After waiting on the Lord earnestly, however, I felt strongly impressed to ride the young, unbroken animal, trusting myself in God's hands.

The Lord had assured me that he would take care of me. The old lady did not want me to ride the colt and seemed to think that I was somewhat obstinate in my decision. Finally, however, she consented.

The girls who went with me were young and mischievous, and when they saw that I did not know how to ride and was very awkward, they began to enjoy my predicament and whipped up their horse just to have fun at my expense. I felt very awkward and scarcely knew how to keep my seat in the saddle. On the way to town the girls asked me if I expected to return to the farm that evening. I said that I did not, to which they replied that they were glad because they wanted a horse apiece coming back, so that they could have a race. There had been a heavy rainfall, and in front of the blacksmith shop at the edge of town was a large mud-puddle in which a hog was wallowing as we came up. Disturbed at our approach, the big animal arose from the puddle, splashing mud and water, and making considerable noise. The gentle horse on which the girls were riding became frightened, jumped to one side, and both girls fell off into the mud. The horse on which I was riding was scarcely frightened at all. He just made a slight movement that loosened my foot from the stirrup. Some one came to my assistance until I could get down. I realized that God had protected me.

One time not long after this a brother was taking me somewhere on a mule. It suddenly came to my mind that I had not trusted God for protection and that I must do so at once as danger was near at hand. In less than five minutes, as we were going through a bit of timber, the mule got scared and began to rear up. Then he tried his best to run with me through the timber. If he had succeeded, no doubt my brains would have been knocked out against a tree. Again an unseen hand seemed to help me, and although the mule kept rearing up and trying to get away, I was uninjured.

At a few other times in my life God has marvelously protected me under similar circumstances. Once the mule on which I was riding became frightened and threw me off. For some time I lay senseless on the ground, but the mule stood still, not moving out of its tracks until I recovered consciousness and crawled away. God answered my prayer, and I was soon all right again. At another time I fell off a horse backwards on my head. A brother and sister who were with me thought that they heard my neck break, but the Lord marvelously protected me, and I was almost as well as usual by evening. At still another time my horse slipped, and I fell off, got caught in the saddle, and was dragged some little distance. At first I called for help, but the sister with me was so frightened that she could not come to my rescue, so I called on God very earnestly, and he helped me out of the dangerous position without any hurt.

Before my brother and I began our work in Chicago, while passing through that city with Brother Kilpatrick and his company, we stopped over to visit Lincoln Park. When the street-car was near the edge of the park, one of the company jumped off, saying, "This is Lincoln Park." I had ridden so little on the street-cars that I did not know the danger of getting on or off while the cars were moving, so I jumped too, thinking that if I did not I should not get to see the park. As I jumped, I kept hold of the car and in consequence was dragged about one hundred yards. When the conductor got his car stopped, he gave me a cursing for being so foolish, but he little realized how ignorant I was. Some of our company were almost sick with fright, thinking that I was killed, but God in his mercy protected me and did not allow me to suffer serious injury.

After we had begun work in the city of Chicago, we went one day out to a little town called Naperville to visit some saints and to hold a meeting. When we came to the depot to start back, my brother found that he had left his Testament at the house where we had been staying, and he went back after it. There was a little suburban station just a short distance from the depot, and the train ran between the two. Our baggage was at the suburban station. I saw the train coming and, supposing of course that it would stop, I went across to the little station to protect our things. The train was a lightning express which did not stop at that station, and the man in charge of the crossing, seeing my danger, began to yell at me to come back. I was too far across to return, and his yelling came near confusing me, so I merely made my escape. The express was not more than a foot away as I stepped off the track.

At different times God has protected me from contageous diseases. While my oldest brother and I were out together in the work, he took the measles. I nursed him during his illness, and others were sure I was taking them. They thought they saw them coming out under my skin, but I was trusting God the best I knew how. Some of the incidents that occurred about this time were rather amusing. About the time I should have been coming down with the measles, Mother Bolds and I attended a meeting in Carthage, Mo. It was a dark night, and we had to cross a little ravine. We lost our way, got into the water, and got drenched. But no bad results came of our wetting, as I was not taking the measles at all. God had protected me.

I had my next experience of this kind at Cornell, Nebraska, when I took care of my brother George during his sickness with the measles. George was very sick. Often after giving him food or water I would find myself tasting of what was left. Then I would think, "I do not want to tempt God; what shall I do? It certainly seems I must have the affliction after being so thoughtless." But I thought of this scripture: "If they drink any deadly thing, it shall not hurt them." I asked the Lord to verify that promise to me.

On two different nights, however, for about two hours each time, the devil seemed to come and try to impose the disease on me. It seemed that I could hear him say, "I will give you the measles; I will give you the measles." "No, you will not," I would say in reply. "I will not have them unless God wants me to have them. You are not going to give them to me." I knew it was Satan that was trying to push the disease on me. The second night it seemed as though I could resist the devil no longer, and I said, "If I do not get help, I can not stand any more." Then the Lord appeared and let me know that I should not be tried any more, and this scripture was fulfilled: "God is faithful, who will not suffer you to be tempted above that ye are able; but will with the temptation also make a way to escape." The enemy disappeared and I did not take the measles.

While in San Diego, California, a brother took George and me over the bay to Cornado Island. Before we started, God impressed me that there was danger ahead and that I should pray earnestly for protection. Thinking that I should not have time before starting, I prayed as I went. Upon reaching the island the brother went to moor the boat, and George called to him, "Are you not afraid to fasten your boat so near to the waves from the main ocean?" He answered that he thought there was no danger.

We spent a very pleasant day on the island and enjoyed the ocean air. When it came time for us to go home, I found that in walking around I had lost my scarf. The brother who was with us said he thought he knew where it was. He told my brother to hold the oars while he went to get the missing article. On his return George went to pass him the oars, but in some way one of them fell into the water. Just then the large waves began to roll in from the open sea and to fill our little boat. It looked as though death was staring us in the face. My brother saw that he could escape; but as he thought that probably the boatman and I would both be drowned, he stayed with us and did all he could to help get the oar. The boat was full of water. We were all drenched and sat there in the water until we got back to the mainland about four miles away.

Although I did not drown, yet probably the wetting would have caused my death had God not answered prayer. How good the Lord was and what a lesson I got! When God impresses us with danger, it is time to lay it to heart and to pray until we know that God has given us the protection we need.

Another incident of this kind occurred in California while we were visiting a place known as the Inner Cave. When the tide was out, people could walk round in this cave and enjoy the scenery; but when the tide was in, the cave was filled with water. We supposed that we knew the time when the tide came into the cave, but we had been misinformed. When we got out into the open air again, it was within five minutes of the time for the return of the tide. Had we remained much longer, we should all have been drowned.

God has certainly been very merciful to me. Many

times has he warned me before meeting with some threatened danger, and always he has protected me from serious harm.

Chapter XVII

My California Trip

For some time a brother in California had been insisting very strongly on our coming to that State to hold meetings. His letters were full of glowing accounts of the beautiful climate and the fine fruit, he thinking that would be an attraction to us. These attractions had no influence upon us. My brother George, Lodema Kaser, and I, who were then together holding a meeting, felt so strongly impressed of the Lord to accept the brother's invitation that we all thought we should go in a week or two. While in earnest prayer, however, God made it clear to me that my mother would need me at home in the near future and that we were not to go to California until a year from the following fall.

During the winter of the year in which we first felt impressed to go to California, mother got erysipelas in the face. At that time my brother and I were out in the work, and my unsaved brother put her in the hands of physicians. While we were holding meetings in Oklahoma, we received a telegram that she was very low, and started for home. At Wichita, Kansas, we telegraphed asking if she was still alive. We got the answer, "Yes, but the doctors say she can't live twelve hours." Up to this time I had the assurance that God would heal her, but when I got the doctor's word, I, like Peter, began looking at the waves and concluded that Mother would die. When I got home, however, and had to trust God, I felt ashamed of myself and decided that I would never again put a doctor's word ahead of God's promises. God spared her life, but the medicine had so reduced her strength that George and I had to stay at home and nurse her for two months.

About two weeks before we were ready to start for California, I saw in a dream a brother coming to give me twenty dollars to help pay my way to California. He said that he had wanted to use the money in some other way, but that God had shown him to use it for pushing his work in southern California. The dream came true in all its details.

Finally our preparations were completed and in November, more than a year after we first felt impressed to go to California, we took train at Newton, Kans. There were seven in our company, Brother and Sister Dansberger, Brother and Sister Gates, Sister Lodema Kaser, and my brother George and I. As we had been brought up in a comparatively level country and had never seen any mountains, the trip was to me a source of wonder and delight. After three days' travel, we reached San Diego and stepped off our train into a land of flowers. Roses were in bloom, geraniums formed a fence around some of the buildings, all nature was in the height of its beauty. We arrived on November 15, just fifteen years to a day from the time I was healed, and exactly five years from the time J. W. Byers reached the Pacific Coast. The contrast between California and the place from which we had come was very marked at this time of the year.

A house in San Diego was given us free of rent and an abundant supply of provisions was brought in by the brethren. Figs were very plentiful in that part of California, and our company enjoyed them very much. If I remember correctly, they bore three crops a year. I learned quite a lesson from the nature of this fruit. Fig-trees do not bloom like most other fruit-trees, but the fig itself pushes out at the end of the twig, just as the leaves begin on a hickory-tree. The tree has no flowers, or bloom. I was told that as the fig grew and ripened it had all the appearance of a bloom. A careful examination proved this statement to be true. The inside of the fig looks like the petals of a beautiful flower. To my mind, this beautifully illustrates the Christian who wears all the blossoms on the inside, and it is not only blossom, but genuine fruit, after all.

I learned another lesson by the ocean-tide. Certainly God's handiwork is displayed in large bodies of water. I could sit and behold his beauty and grandeur hour after hour and never grow tired. In fact, it seemed that I could see the hand of God, traces of his wonderful works and creation, until I was awed into silence and felt like saying as Job did of old, "When the Almighty speaks, I will put my hand on my mouth." The lesson I learned was this:

When the tide is out, the rocks along the shore, covered with seaweed and moss, present an unsightly appearance; but when the tide comes in, these unsightly things are all covered with water, which present the appearance of a sea of glass. When the grace of God is low in our soul, the unseemly parts of human nature are on exhibition; but when the grace of God floods the soul, then Christ is on exhibition and the unseemly parts are hidden away.

Another lesson that might be drawn is this: The coming in of the tide might be compared to the trials and the tests that flood our souls, and the going out of the tide to the subsiding of the trials, which, like the going out of the tide, leaves behind pearls and shells and other beautiful things. The beauties of the Christian life are brought to view by the waves of trial that sweep over the souls.

We went out into the country, visited the saints, and enjoyed the orange-groves for about two weeks. In the ocean we saw God's hand exhibited in might and power. Here we saw God's hand none the less, although exhibited in gentleness and beneficence. The orange-trees were a beautiful sight. They were loaded with fruit in various stages of development. On the very same tree there would be blossoms and oranges ranging in size from the small green ones to the large ripe ones.

Once while we were near the ocean, we thought it a good opportunity to visit the man-of-war that was stationed about half a mile out from the shore.

We went out to it in a little sail-boat. As we were passing under a pier, the oarsman dropped one of his oars in the water and regained possession of it only with a great deal of difficulty. One of our party, a sister, becoming greatly frightened because of our danger, took hold of one of the pier-posts and held to it with all her might. In the meantime the brother had gotten hold of his oar and was trying to make the boat move. He soon saw that there was some hindrance, and, looking around, found the sister holding to the pier-post. When asked why she was doing that, she answered, "I am afraid we shall drown." "Woman," he said, "if you will not let go of that post, you will drown every one of us." I have often thought how much like this sister some Christians act. They are afraid they will be overwhelmed, but they hold to something on the shore, to the pier-post of the world or of their own ideas, which makes it impossible for them to get out where it is smooth sailing. Some of these, however, are sincere and honest in heart, finally wake up to what they are doing, say that they have Christ as their pilot, take their hands off, and get out on the open sea of life where the waters are calmed by the Spirit of the Lord.

While we were in San Diego there came to us a woman in destitute circumstances. She and her husband had recently come from another part of the country and had not yet succeeded in finding work. They were almost at the point of starvation, and so she came to us to borrow some money. The woman herself professed salvation, but I think knew but little of the truth. Her husband was a sinner. She told us that her husband was out of work and that although he was unsaved he would not eat anything for breakfast that morning for fear there would not be enough left to keep his children from starving until he could get work. We were much moved by the compassion he had shown for his little ones, and thought how much more compassion our Heavenly Father has for his children. The Word says, "Like as a father pitieth his children, so the Lord pitieth them that fear him." We felt led to divide the flour, meat, fruit, and butter we had on hands. Before the day was over, there was brought to us from the country ten miles away more provisions than we had given away. The destitute family had enough to live on until the husband got work, which was only a few days later. "Give, and it shall be given unto you; good measure pressed down, and shaken together, and running over."

It has been said that every false doctrine that starts from the eastern part of the United States has a through ticket to the Pacific Coast. We could readily believe this statement. California seemed to be a hot-bed of false doctrine. It was difficult to get any truth to the people or to get them free from the false doctrines of which they had partaken.

From San Diego we went to Los Angeles, where we lived in a tent and held meetings in a large tabernacle, with fairly good crowds. The gospel message was not without effect, but we found the people so filled with false doctrine that it was almost impossible to get the truth to them. Even the brother who was so anxious for us to come to California was scattering false doctrine wherever he went. Among other things, he opposed women's preaching. God put us on his trail and kept us after him until the enemy was thoroughly rebuked, and he humbled himself and asked forgiveness.

While in this place, most of our little company was under arrest for about three hours for preaching on the street. Some one had reported us to the police and had misrepresented what we were doing. Some of our company enjoyed being under arrest very much, feeling that they had a foretaste of a martyr's experience. When they were released, they came back to the tent rejoicing and praising God that they were counted worthy to suffer for Jesus' sake. This did not end our street-meetings; many more were held during our stay in California.

During our stay at Los Angeles, a blacksmith, a brother in the church, while shoeing a horse, got a severe kick in the head. His condition seemed very serious. He came to the tent before meeting began and requested prayer, saying that after prayer he would return to his tent, as he was feeling pretty bad. God wonderfully answered prayer and healed him so that he was able to sit up during the meeting. About three days later one of our company was in his shop and asked him how he was getting along. The reply was that his head was all right, but that a little wound on his hand unnoticed before was giving him some trouble. "But," he added, "I thank the Lord that it is no worse." The brother replied, "Can't you thank the Lord that it is as it is?" The blacksmith stood thoughtful for a moment and then said, "Yes; why shouldn't I thank the Lord that it is just as it is?" The words had scarcely left his mouth before the healing power of God came and made his hand perfectly well.

Many other incidents occurred while we were there that space will not permit me to mention here. We remained a little over three months, doing some work in the country, although we were out of town only a few days. At the close of the meeting we moved to Alameda, one of the suburbs of San Francisco. The town at that time covered considerable ground, but had very few large buildings in it. At this place also we lived in a tent as before and held meetings in a large tabernacle. Services were held almost every night, and much precious seed was sown.

One day a sister called on us: She said: "Your brother said in his sermon a few nights since that we should bear one another's burdens. How can we do this if we do not open our hearts to others and tell what our burdens are? Do you think it would be all right for me to open my heart to you and tell you my burden?"

"Certainly," I answered, "if your soul is burdened." "I have," said she, "a heavy burden to carry. Now, my husband no longer loves me, but he has given all his affections to my sister. They are likely to elope at any time, and my heart is broken. In fact, the grief and trouble I have endured have brought on heart-trouble." As she finished her story, we asked, "Is there anything we can do? We should be glad to do anything to help you bear your burden. Do you think it would be a good idea to have a day of fasting and prayer?" "Yes," said she, "I think it would do good." We told her to set the day, and she chose the next Friday. On that day we all fasted and prayed, especially for this man. It was not over two weeks before God got hold of his heart and gloriously saved him. A happier person than this sister I do not think you could have found. It seemed that she could not cease praising God and thanking us.

In order to defray the expenses at home, she raised poultry for the market. To show her gratitude to us, she brought chickens, eggs, and other things for our use until we were afraid she was really robbing herself. She fairly loaded us with good things, and when we called her attention to how generously she was supplying our needs and told her we were afraid she was doing too much, she would say, "Oh, no; I never can repay you for what you have done for my family." We would say, "Do not try too hard to repay us, as it was God who did the work for you." I heard of the man not many years ago, and was still sweetly saved.

In our company were Brother and Sister Gates and their three children, who had come with us from Kansas. Not only had Brother and Sister Gates helped us financially, but they had been as a father and mother to us all. They were now about to leave us, and they seemed somewhat burdened lest we should suffer need, as the people had not yet been supplying our needs very much. Of course, the reason why God had not been supplying us otherwise up to this time was not hard to find. The Lord knew that they were supplying our need and that we required no additional help from others.

Before leaving us, the sister said, "What are you going to do after we are gone?" I answered: "The Lord has always been a present help in time of need. You and Brother Gates have been very helpful to us, for which we are thankful; but, sister, you must remember that is was God working through you. If God had not been blessing your souls, doubtless we should not have received special help from you. So, after all, the help you gave us came from God. I am sure when you are gone the Lord will not forsake us."

It seemed, however, that the Lord wanted to encourage them before their departure by beginning to manifest his care for us. A baker, a stranger to us, came one morning before we were up and left half a dozen loaves of nice bread on the table in one of our tents that we used as a kitchen. The next day Sister Gates said, "Well, you have some nice bread." The following day the same number of loaves were left and the sister remarked, "I think I shall accept some of that bread to take on our journey, and I won't have to bake as I expected." Again, the third morning the usual number of loaves were left in our tent, and Sister Gates remarked: "I wish we knew who that man is, so that we could tell him to stop bringing bread. You will soon have more bread on hands than you will know what to do with." I answered, "God wants to show you how he will take care of us after you are gone." When we found out who the baker was, we asked him to leave a smaller amount of bread for us, as our company was not so large as it had been. He continued, however, to bring us bread, also buns, cookies, and cake, all of which were very much appreciated. His donations continued during most of the time we were at this place.

One of our company dropped a tract at a house near the outskirts of the city. This tract was the means of the salvation of the woman who found it. Her husband, who was a dairyman and sold milk in a certain part of the city, told my brother if he would come to a certain place which he passed daily, he could have three pints of milk every day. Two or three days before Brother and Sister Gates left us, provisions of all kinds - fruit, meat, and even baked goods - came pouring in. We had already decided that, as Brother and Sister Gates were soon going to leave us, our company would all take their dinner together on Sunday. Our table was loaded down. The meal looked more like a wedding-dinner than the meal of a few humble traveling preachers. When Brother and Sister Gates saw how bountifully God had provided for us, they were delighted and satisfied.

A sister who had come to us shortly after our arrival at Alameda told us that we had to be very careful and economical with the provisions, because we should not be so bountifully supplied here as we had been at San Diego and Los Angeles, because at those other places the church had been taught to give. "There are but few saints here," she said, "and they do not know their duty, so we need not expect large contributions." We replied, "Even if they do not know their duty, God is just the same, and they that trust him shall not be confounded." I do not know that we were better supplied at any other place in the State.

During our stay at Alameda, we went over to San Francisco and sat on the porch of the Cliff House overlooking the sea and watched the herds of seals that were playing on a little island out in the ocean about a quarter of a mile. They acted like a party of mischievous children. One of the animals would throw another into the ocean, and the one in the water would come up dripping. As we watched them, we could imagine that they entered into the fun of the sport and really felt mischievous.

At Fresno, the next place in our itinerary, a widow provided us with a furnished house, rent free, with fruit in the cellar and everything needed to make us comfortable. We remembered at this time that Elijah was provided for by a widow.

In one part of the house was a woman tenant who soon proved to be our enemy and tried to persecute us. While we were having worship, she would make fun of us and disturb us in every way she could. We made up our minds we would obey the Lord in "putting coals of fire on her head." We sought every opportunity to show little kindnesses. At first our efforts were all in vain; she spurned every advance we made. Finally, she took sick, and we went in and asked the privilege of helping her. At first she rejected, but finally consented, and we went to work to prepare her food and to do whatever else was necessary to make her comfortable. Our kindness reached her heart. After she recovered, she showed some signs of gratitude, and we improved every opportunity to accomplish our design of over-coming evil with good. At last she was won to the truth, sought the Lord, found him precious to her soul, and was ever after our firm friend. It was only about three years ago, I think, that she sent me one dollar in a letter.

The people in Fresno had heard but little of the present truth. There was one brother living in the town, however, who had done a little house-to-house work, lending books, visiting the sick, etc. Among others, he had made the acquaintance of two aged sisters, one of whom was a habitual user of morphine. She was a doctor's widow and had acquired the habit by taking morphine as a remedy shortly after their marriage. As these old ladies talked with the brother (Martin) and as they learned of what the Lord had done for the souls and bodies of different people, there was awakened in their hearts a desire to trust the Lord for deliverance.

One day a sister of our company and I had planned to do some calling. At this time we were in need of such provisions as butter, milk, eggs, etc. The sister thought, therefore, that we had better go to a sister who we felt sure would help us in our time of need. I felt more inclined to go and see the woman who was addicted to the morphine-habit, and accordingly we turned our steps in that direction. The two old ladies were much pleased to have us come, and the one who was bound by the morphine-habit desired very much to be delivered. Before we left, they wanted to know if we had a cow. We told them no, and without our asking they supplied us with all the milk, butter, eggs, and buttermilk we needed.

As we left, they requested that we should come back and pray for the sister's deliverance. Their brother also came after me the following Monday morning to go and have prayer for her. For nearly forty years she had been addicted to the morphine habit and had been given up by the doctors who had treated her. Four or five years before this, spots such as usually come on the skin of those who have long been users of morphine, appeared on her skin, showing that she was beyond the reach of medical skill. I went there, prayed for her, but felt that her case was so serious that there would be a prolonged fight, so I returned and sent Sister Kaser. She remained at the house for twelve days. For three or four days it was a life and death fight. Then the old lady began to come out from under the influence of the drug, to throw off the effects, and in twelve days she was like another person. Things that she ate began to taste natural, and her health improved. God had wrought a perfect deliverance.

It was during our stay at this place that we had the privilege of visiting the park in which are the giant redwoods of California. For thirty miles on the trip we went in a carriage, and then we took a large mountain-wagon drawn by two pair of horses. As we ascended the mountain to the park, we passed through vegetation in various conditions. At Fresno, where we began our journey, no rain falls and vegetation grows only by means of irrigation. As we ascended, we came first to where there was a small amount of moisture, and the grass was just beginning to make its appearance. As we got further up the mountain, the vegetation was more abundant and flowers were growing here and there. The further we went the greener was the foliage, the stronger the growth, and when we reached the height we were in a grove of giant trees.

Just before reaching the park we were threatened with a danger that we least expected. During the summer, government troops camped in the park, and as we came up the narrow road, we met the army-wagons coming toward us. The road was so narrow, with the sheer side of the mountain rising on one side and a precipice on the other, that to pass these wagons was impossible. We had to wait until the government-wagons passed before resuming our trip.

When we approached the grove of redwoods, the stumps looked so large that I supposed the trees would be larger than they really were and hence I was quite disappointed in their size. My disappointment, of course, was due to the effect on my senses, for the trees were really immense. I walked through a hollow log through which a lady had ridden on horseback some time before. Later, I stood on top of this log and it seemed as if I were standing on top of a house. The largest tree we measured was 103 feet in circumference at its base. The name of this monster was General Washington. People had climbed far up its sides and carved their names. In order to get a good idea of the height of these great trees, one has to lie on the ground near the base and look up. Through the roots of one tree that was visited, a beautiful spring of ice-cold water bubbled up. The spring came up through a decayed opening in the root of the tree.

California is much different from the Eastern States. In the low lands of California there is no lightning nor thunder. The rain comes so gently that sometimes one has to look out-of-doors to see whether or not it is raining. But in the mountains the thunder and lightning are very sharp. Then, too, the difference in temperature between the lowlands and the highlands seems remarkable. At Fresno the thermometer registered 109 after sundown, while on the mountain the temperature was only 60. In California the vegetable growth differs greatly from that in the East. In the East our common elders die every other year; in California they grow to be as large around as a man's body. In the East the castor-bean is an annual; in California it is a tree, many of them larger than a man's body. We had tomatoes in mid-winter from vines that had been bearing for many months, and we saw beets that had grown year after year until they were of great size, in comparison with those of eastern section.

While at Fresno we took a trip in carriages across the country to Farmersville, a small town in the interior, about forty miles away. We also attended a camp-meeting at Tulare, where we met Brother and Sister Brundage and other saints.

In the month of March, after being in California a year and four months, we took the southern route and returned East by way of Arizona. We stopped at Phoenix and held a two weeks' meeting with good success. One evening I visited a sick sister, who seemed to be suffering considerably. She did not ask for prayer, and I did not volunteer to pray for her. As I left, her little three-year-old child heard her say that she wished Sister Cole had prayed for her while there, as she wanted to be healed and go to meeting that night. "Mama," said the little one, "I will pray for you," and she stepped up and put her little hands on her mama's head. After prayer she said, "Mama, are you better now?" "No." "All right, I will pray for you again." Again she asked the Lord to make her mama well. "Mama, aren't you better now?" "No, I feel as bad as ever." "Well, I will pray for you again." By this time the mother saw that the child had more faith than she. She decided to exercise every bit of faith she had.

After the little girl had prayed the third time, she said, "Mama, aren't you better now?" The mother answered, "Yes, I believe the Lord heals me." She got up and dressed herself, and sure enough she was well.

At the street-meetings we held in Phoenix, there were present Indians and a number of foreigners of different nationalities. While in this town we had the privilege of visiting our old friends, Brother and Sister Pine, who were then living a few miles out of the city. Both we and they were much delighted to meet again. A day or two more of traveling on the railway, and we were again among familiar scenes, which seemed very dear to us after so long an absence.

Chapter XVIII

Visiting Relatives in the East

After our return from California I found that my body was much worn by our labors in that State. I therefore rested for a few weeks; then in company with my brother George, I attended a number of camp-meetings that summer. A little later in the year we went to visit relatives in Ohio and Indiana, stopping on the way to hold a few meetings in the city of Chicago. On this trip we visited also my mother's old home in Carroll County, Ohio, and while there saw many things, which, although new to us, seemed familiar because of her oft-repeated stories in regard to them. Although we had a pleasant time, because of the sociability and kindness of the people we visited, yet our hearts were saddened that we found none of our relatives enjoying a clear experience of salvation.

George returned to the West and I remained for sometime longer with an uncle, Mother's brother. I did what I could while I was there to lead these dear ones to see the full light of Christianity, but I do not know whether or not I accomplished anything. The time was now drawing near for me to return to the West, and I did not have money enough to pay my way. I felt ashamed to let my relatives know anything about it, as I had been telling them of God's goodness in providing for me and trying to teach them to trust God for all things. I had hoped that George, who knew something of my financial straits, would send me some money. I was expecting to hear from him, but when he did write, he sent only a postal card. My uncle's folks had spoken in a way that showed doubt as to whether I had money enough to pay my car-fare, but I had told them that I was trusting the Lord and that he would provide.

I prayed very earnestly and the Lord seemed to bring to my mind an incident connected with the crossing of the Jordan by the children of Israel. They had to prove God by stepping into the edge of the water before he saw fit to make the waters roll back, thus opening a path for them through the river. I was impressed that God wanted to test me and that I should have to be willing to go to the depot without the money. Uncle did not take me to the depot, but found a chance for me to ride with a neighbor. At the depot I met a man who professed to be a saint, and I wondered if he would not help me pay my way. He had intimated that he might help me. But he did not ask me whether I needed any money, nor did he offer to give me any. I was asking God earnestly what to do, and I had just about decided to buy a ticket to a point as far as my money would pay and then to trust God for the rest of my fare, when, looking up, I saw in the distance some one coming through the heat, and as he drew nearer, I recognized him as Uncle.

He had not come to the depot with me, as he was afraid it would be too hard for him to walk back, but now he was coming. I wondered why, and when he got near me I said, "O Uncle! why did you come through this heat?" The tears began to roll down his face, and he said, "Mary, I was afraid you didn't have enough money." "Uncle," I said, "I guess God showed you, for I didn't have enough. I lack about fifty cents." He said, "When I was at your home, your brothers were so good to help me that I felt it was my duty to see that you had enough money to pay your way." "Uncle," I said, "I won't need more than fifty cents." "Here is a dollar; take it." "No, you give me just fifty cents." He did so, and I had just a few cents more than enough to pay my fare.

I can almost see the dear old soul yet coming through the heat almost exhausted - and then to think how good the Lord was to help me in this time of need! The thought of the Lord's kindness melted me to tears, and I thanked him over and over. This incident shows, too, that many times a kind deed long forgotten is rewarded at a later time when help is much needed. Let us not forget to "scatter deeds of kindness for our reaping by and by."

A short time after this we went on a visit to the old home at Windsor, Mo. The night after we came an electric storm passed over the little town, accompanied with a high wind and torrents of rain.

While the storm was at its height, lightning struck the belfry of the Baptist chapel, two doors from our house. The meeting-house was soon in flames, and the high wind hurled great pieces of burning timbers over our house, and for a while there seemed great danger of its taking fire too. Mother was quite uneasy, but God made us to know that he would protect us.

While on this visit, George and I went about twenty miles distance in a buggy to visit a brother and a sister and their families. While on our return trip we stopped at the little town of Lincoln to water our horses, and George took the bits out of the horse's mouth to let him drink. The animal became frightened at the sound of the wind-mill where we were watering, and began to run, and as there were no bits in his mouth, the lines in my hands were useless. My brother undertook to hold the horse, but under the circumstances he could not do so. He saw that my life was in danger, and in trying to rescue me he got wound up in the lines and was hurt quite a little. I was thrown out of the buggy and dragged about a hundred yards and badly injured internally. When George got to me, I was unconscious, but I soon came to myself. Then we both called earnestly on God, who answered prayer. We were both sufficiently relieved so that when the horse got over its fright and the buggy was repaired, we started on our journey of seventeen miles home. We thanked God that the sky was clouded over; thus God held his big umbrella over us and gave us protection from the heat, as we were both very sick and in danger of fainting.

I found later that the injury I had received in the runaway was more serious than we had at first thought. I trusted God as best I could for my healing, and we soon started on our way to Neosho Falls, Kansas, to attend a camp-meeting. Within seven days after I was hurt, I was scarcely able to be up at all. My nerves were in such a condition that I could scarcely bear any noise at all, not even the sound of a person's voice. Because of the weakness and the pain I suffered, I missed most of the meeting and lay in bed for about three weeks after the meeting closed. The injury had so affected my brain that I was not capable of grasping God's promises for my healing. About this time I had a dream. I was in a large ship that was in a sinking condition. I was not in the water, but was clinging desperately to the side of the vessel. We called for help, and a tug-boat came to our rescue. Fearing I could not hold on much longer, I called to them to hurry. They replied that they must rescue Sister Martin first. I awoke, and the Lord made me to know that, owing to the condition of my brain, I could not myself obtain healing, and that I should ask the church to help bear the burden. So I got the church at Neosho Falls to fast and pray, and we also had the saints in Moundsville to agree with us in prayer. God heard prayer, healed my body, and my brother and I soon started on our journey east again.

On our way we stopped at home and stayed over one night. One of the sisters in that neighborhood begged me to remain and rest a whole year, saying if I did not I would soon be in my grave. My reply was: "I need more than a rest. God wants me to go. He can help me where I am going as well as at home. Pray for me, sister, that God will grant me all the healing I yet need." She promised me she would. From this time on I gained rapidly, but it was a month or more before I was as strong as usual.

On our way east we went through Kentucky and held some meetings with Brother Kilpatrick. George took the eczema, and after these meetings his condition became serious. For about two months he suffered greatly. During this time he could not sit down, but had to either stand or lie. Before he recovered, we got a call to come to Chicago. We started, but George was so feeble that I did not know whether or not he would live until we got to our destination. The brother with whom we had been staying insisted that we stay longer, but we felt God urging us on, so we went.

Chapter XIX

Mission Work in Chicago

On arriving in Chicago, we found Brother T - , who had charge of the work in the city, at 1612 Prairie Ave. For nearly a year my brother and I assisted him in the work, and then, as he insisted that we become responsible for the work in a general way, we took charge.

When we first went to Chicago, we were not just sure what God wanted us to do. The first winter I helped hold meetings for homeless men in the slum district. As a class, these people were so deep in sin that it was hard to reach them. A few, however, did get a real experience of salvation; but it was difficult for them to keep saved, and when they would give up, they would not stop until they had gone into the grossest kind of sin. Some of them would get converted again and again, only to be overcome by the tempter. Their characters had been so weakened by indulging in sin and giving way to their appetites that it seemed hard for them to become established. It took a great deal of patience and labor to get any of them established. The religious career of many of them was very brief, but others struggled on for a long time. No doubt some became thoroughly established and remained true to the Lord.

Mary Cole

This work was not very satisfactory to us. True, the souls of these people are as precious in the sight of God as the souls of any other people, but we soon saw that the energy expended upon these people of the slums would, if directed toward people in the great middle walks of life, accomplish far more in the salvation of souls. Gospel workers, if the Lord leads you to take up slum-work, be sure to obey the Lord, but be equally sure that you don't attempt slum-work unless God is leading you.

As the work was not satisfactory to us, my brother rented a house for five years as a missionary home. The monthly rent was $25, and it was wonderful how God answered prayer and brought the means to pay the rent. Many times our support would come from a distance. For two or three years before we came to the city, Brother T - had held meetings every Sunday afternoon in the Masonic Temple. The rent for the room in which we held services in the temple for two and one-half hours each week, was for a time $15 a month, and later $16. Besides the meeting in the Temple, we had cottage-meetings in different parts of the city.

Besides renting the home in which most of the workers lived, my brother rented for a year a house to serve as a home for workers in the slum district, paying a monthly rental of $60. As my brother was ignorant of what he was getting into, the Lord seemed to humor him for two or three months by providing the money for the rent of this building. Then my brother got into trouble. He prayed earnestly for money to pay the rent on this building, but his prayers would not go through. Heaven seemed closed against him. After making several efforts in this way, for a while without avail, my brother said that if he could not get his prayers through for money to pay the rent, he would pray that God would make the landlord willing to give up the lease. His prayers were heard, the landlord surrendered the lease, and George got out of his difficulty. Subsequent events showed that the Lord was willing to provide money for us in abundance as long as we acted in accordance with his divine plan for us.

In consideration of the facts that we paid our $40 a month for rent on our home and meeting-place, and that we enjoyed but limited privileges in holding meetings, my brother felt impressed before the five years were out that the Lord wanted us to build a home which should be permanent and which should be the property of the church. The work was begun in March, 1903, and by the blessing of God and the cooperation of the church in general, the home and chapel were both finished by Christmas. The greater part of the work was donated, one experienced carpenter giving over $600 worth of labor.

Our work in the city was a school of trust. We trusted the Lord for food, for raiment, for rent, and for everything else that we needed. Sometimes when I would have a little money laid by, an opportunity would come to use it, and I would think,

"I don't want to give this up, for I may need it later." Then the voice of the Spirit would say to me, "If you don't keep your purse open and use the means you have, God will not supply you." I obeyed God, and he never allowed me to be confounded. Many times when we did not have sufficient food for the whole day, we would get down and ask God to send either money or food. It was marvelous how our prayers were answered, and that from sources from which we should have least expected help. The Lord wonderfully encouraged our hearts in this way.

When we were building the home and chapel, a number of the workers felt led to purpose a certain sum to be paid in a year's time. The first year my purpose was $100, to be paid before December 31. I got just enough to finish paying it December 30. The workers were all encouraged in like manner. The next year some of them suggested that, as God had helped them through so marvelously the first year, we should purpose twice as much. I received sufficient money to pay the $200 by Thanksgiving, a month sooner than I had paid the $100 the year before.

We often had to trust the Lord for car-fare, and many times it came to us in remarkable ways. One day one of the sisters started out to make a call in the city with only enough money to pay her fare one way. While she was sitting in the car, she looked down into her lap and there lay a quarter. How it got there was a mystery. Sometimes even strangers passing us on the street would feel impressed to hand us enough money to pay our fares. Again, some of the workers while trusting the Lord would find just the amount needed.

The Lord showed us here in the city as he did while we were in California, that he wanted us not only to appreciate and enjoy the blessings sent us, but also to pass some of our blessings to those who were needy, and that in so doing we should be blessed as well as those who gave to us. Brethren, God's plan is an unselfish one. If we expect to grow in grace and to develop in trust and in other of his precious graces, we must unselfishly impart what God gives to us. "Freely ye have received, freely give." "He that watereth shall be watered again." "The willing and the obedient shall eat the good of the land." If we withhold blessings from others, whether it be means or any other help that we can afford them, we ourselves shall be losers, and they will be deprived of their rights.

Some little time after we located in the city we had our mother come to live with us. She had been a widow for some years. I counted it a happy privilege that I should be allowed to care for her in her old days. I had long desired to care for her and took advantage of the first opportunity of having her come to us. I had also desired that in her old days she should not lose her mind as some old people do, and that she should enjoy a good long life. My prayers have been answered and my hopes realized. [Footnote: Nearly a year after the above account was written, on October 22, 1914, Mother died at the age of ninety-two years. She had the right use of her mind until the last. After she had lost the power to see and hear distinctly, she would recognize me by a sign to which we had agreed and would call my name, and even after speech had failed, she still attempted to say, "Mary."] We had been in Chicago only about a year when news came from Hammond, Louisiana, that my oldest brother, Jeremiah, had died at that place, October 13, 1899. While we were in California, Jeremiah came to that State and held meetings, although he was with us only a short time. For some years before his death his health had not been very good, and in the fall of 1899 he went to the South for the third time to winter. While he was holding meetings nor far from Hammond, Louisiana, October 1, he became suddenly sick while preaching and had to leave the pulpit in the middle of his discourse.

Bro. F. M. Williamson, at whose home he was staying, begged to be allowed to write or telegraph to his folks, but Jeremiah said, "No, my illness will last but a few days, and it is no use to worry my folks." He lingered until October 13, when he died. Brother Williamson, who was with him until the end, said that my brother had the confidence of everybody in that part of the country and that he died a triumphant death. Shortly before my brother's death a letter was sent us saying that he was very sick, but it did not reach us until several days after his burial.

Before going to Chicago, we had worked almost altogether in small towns and in the country. Of course, the work in such a large city as Chicago was quite different. Nevertheless, we were glad for the experience we had had and of the chance we now had for putting it in practise and of making improvement. We learned, however, that the souls of men are much the same, whether they live in a city or in the country, and that God gives his ministers authority over evil spirits wherever they may be found.

When we took the Chicago work in charge, there was in the congregation a certain man who had gotten under a wrong spirit and had led others away with him, thus causing trouble and dissension. The false spirit seemed to be strongly entrenched and very hard to get rid of. This man of whom we have spoken, and whom, for want of a better name, we shall designate as Brother B - , sent word to quite a large number of the saints in the city to be present at the meeting-place on a certain Sunday evening, as he would occupy the pulpit from five until six after the regular meeting closed. Some of our company were out of the city during that week, and on Saturday night a fearful snow-storm came, continuing on into Sunday.

I wished very much that those workers who were out of the city should return for the Sunday evening service, as I saw that we were going to have to meet the enemy in a very bold way. When I awoke Sunday morning, however, the Lord made me know that I must be willing to face the enemy with him alone, and this song rang in my heart:

> "I'll go where You want me to go, dear Lord;
> I'll say what You want me to say."

God was my perfect sufficiency. Some of the members of the congregation who might be included under the Scriptural term "lambs" stood by me like warriors. Two of them sat in the pulpit with me, one on each side to hold my hands, as it were. God had warned me in a dream of the enemy's attack and had shown me some things that were very helpful in that very hour. In my dream I had seen the enemy in the form of a ferocious animal approaching to destroy God's children. We were in a large pavilion which was entered by a large open door. In my dream I thought that God told me to go and shut that door. I started to obey, and when I got near it, the animal was about to enter, but God made me to know that he would help me through and enable me to get the door shut. As I shut the large door, the Lord showed me another little door, saying, "Go and shut that too."

On the Sunday of which I am speaking, when I really had to face the enemy, God gave me as a subject for my sermon various instances in the history of the church where the enemy had attacked God's children and work and where God himself had defended them and defeated the enemy. I spoke of how Joseph's brethren plotted to take his life and finally sold him into Egypt as a slave; of how God made him a prince and a ruler over his brethren and finally their savior and benefactor. I spoke of Jesus - how the Jews killed him, put his body into a sepulcher, closed it with a great stone, sealed it with the king's seal; how the Lord defeated their purpose, arose from the dead, and ascended to the right hand of God. Right in the middle of the sermon God showed me what he meant by shutting the big door and made me to know that I must expose and renounce the one under the spirit of the devil who was trying to undermine the work. He showed me, furthermore, that another man who was helping him was the little door and that he wanted me to denounce him also.

As I began denouncing the spirit of error that had crept into the congregation, the poor deluded ones clamored for a chance to defend themselves, but God showed me that I should give no place to the devil. I advised all the true children of the Lord to leave the meeting-place at the proper time, and not to listen to the enemy's pouring out against God's work and cause. Most of the people took my advice and left at the proper time. Just a few backsliders and chronic grumblers remained to hear Brother B - 's message. I can not tell you how God used this victory to encourage and strengthen my soul. He seemed to humor and pet me all the next day and to bring it to me again and again that he was pleased with me. I seemed to hear him say again and again, "I am well pleased with you."

One of the company who had been with us for some time, did not seem to be making the development as a worker that we had expected him to make. He came so far short of our anticipation that we were tempted at times to conclude that we were mistaken in encouraging him to remain in the work with us. The enemy, of course, worked hard to discourage him and we were beginning to think that perhaps it would be well to discourage his remaining longer with us. When I prayed earnestly over the matter, however, the Lord made me understand that this was a worthy child of his and that in his soul there was a trueness and faithfulness not to be found in every worker. The Lord showed me that if we would exercise patience with him, development would come in good time. The outcome has been all that could be desired. For a number of years this brother's name has been familiar throughout the church, and he is still holding some of the most responsible places.

At another time this same brother was going through a fiery trial. God no doubt was permitting the trial to broaden him and to develop him for future usefulness. What he was enduring, however, became a severe trial to me. Finally it seemed as though I had endured about all that I could, so I said to him one day, "Either you or I will have to leave. I can't stand this any more." He did not answer me, but went away by himself and asked God to give me more compassion.

Dear brothers and sisters in the ministry, right here I would sound a note of warning. Let us be careful when a young worker comes among us. Even if he does not seem promising at first, let us have patience with him and give him a chance; let him prove himself. Let us give him all the encouragement we can and do what we can to help develop him. Perhaps you can help such a one by telling him some of God's dealings with you and how he helped you out of difficulty, how he tided you over and lifted you above discouragements, how he brushed away the dark clouds. Do not be too quick to conclude, "Well, I don't believe God had his hand upon that person, after all," for we might find ourselves working against God instead of being coworkers with him.

We had not been in the city a great while until we had more calls than we could fill. People wrote asking us to call on their friends to see if we could not get the truth to them. We were called to visit places that were by no means inviting. We also had calls from suburban towns and other near-by places, and at times we were led to hold meetings for a week or two in places outside the city. Surely we fulfilled the scripture, "Sow beside all waters." We soon learned from experience that not all who came to the home telling pitiful stories of need were deserving of help. Sometimes after giving provisions and even money, we learned that our charity had been misapplied. We soon learned that it was wise to find out whether we were helping the worthy poor or impostors.

After the chapel was built, opportunities for reaching souls greatly increased. We now had meetings whenever we chose, especially on Sunday evenings, Thursday afternoon and evening, with good attendance of saints and truth-seekers. Our expenses, too, were greatly lessened in this way, especially at the time of the yearly assemblies. One year the rental of the building in which the assembly was held, was, I think, $300 for ten days. Before a certain assembly the saints had contributed freely to provide money for the coming assembly. Shortly before the meeting began the treasury was robbed of over $200.

During the ten years I spent in the Chicago work, I witnessed many wonderful deliverances from sin, from disease, and from evil spirits. The account of these experiences would of itself make a large volume; I can mention only a few here. Sister Pearl Horman, who came to the home, was taken very sick with fever. Her case was very serious, the fever being very high. The Lord rebuked the fever and in a short time she was well. Sister Myra Barrett came to a meeting we were having in the chapel one night, and remained all night in the home. Before morning she had an attack of erysipelas in the face, accompanied by a high fever. The Lord put his rebuke on the disease and not many days later she was able to resume her duties in an office in the city.

In answer to a call from Joliet, Illinois, we went to that place and anointed a brother who was very sick with the quinsy. In answer to the prayer of faith, God wonderfully healed him. One winter night a call came from the suburbs of the city for some one to come and anoint a child suffering from a violent attack of pneumonia. The snow lay deep on the ground and the weather was very cold. My brother and I answered the call. As the night was far spent, the street-cars were no longer running in the direction we had to go, and so we had to walk over a mile facing the wintry storm. God answered prayer in behalf of the child. It was better before we left next morning and was soon entirely well.

At another time we were called upon to pray for a boy who had appendicitis. The doctors who examined him said that without an operation he could not possibly live, but his father, being a saint, desired prayer. Brother Reardon and I anointed the boy, prayed the prayer of faith, and the boy was healed. God got the glory that time instead of the doctor, not to speak of the saving of a great deal of suffering and a heavy doctor-bill.

My mother was in the home at the time Sister Barrett was healed of erysipelas. About ten years before this time Mother had the same affliction, and it came near taking her life. As a result, she had an especial dread of this disease. Before coming to the home, Mother had not been able to wholly trust the Lord for healing, but when she came to live with us, she decided to trust the Lord. But when she saw Sister Barrett having such a severe attack of erysipelas, she became a little alarmed and used something as a preventive, not realizing that it would hinder her faith. In nine days she had a severe attack of erysipelas. For a number of days she had quite a fight of faith, and we sent telegrams to The Trumpet Office twice. God in his mercy rebuked the disease, and she recovered rapidly for one of her age. Although she was past eighty-one, her recovery was much more rapid than it had been ten years before, when she had trusted the doctor.

Sometime after mother was entirely well, we found the little preventive she had in her pocket and asked her about it. She confessed with tears that she had been using the preventive. We encouraged her to trust God fully for protection as well as for everything else. From that time forward she has been able to put her trust wholly in God. Some say that people get too old to trust the Lord, but in her case the older she gets, the more childlike becomes her trust in God.

A brother Jones, now of West Virginia, came to the home from a place where there was an epidemic of smallpox. He was just beginning to take the disease; in fact, a pimple or two had already appeared. He would take spells of being deathly sick, a common occurrence before breaking out with smallpox. The brother was innocent in coming to the home in that condition, thinking that he had been exposed to the chicken-pox and that he was just coming down with a bad case of that disease. He trusted the Lord wholly for healing, and we all united our faith with his against the disease.

The Monday following his arrival he, in company with my brother and others of the saints, went to the camp-meeting at Moundsville, W. Va. That same evening God made us who were left at the home to understand very definitely that the brother had the smallpox and that we should pray very earnestly that God would keep him from breaking out until the nature of the disease could be discovered and the brother be put under quarantine to protect the camp-meeting. Our greatest fears were that the whole camp would be quarantined. The Lord encouraged our hearts to continue in prayer that he would overrule the whole matter. In a few days they found out that Brother Jones was taking the smallpox, and they put him under quarantine. Very soon afterward he broke out. God had answered our prayers to keep him from breaking out, and he also protected us at the home and those at the camp-meeting. Our God is able to protect in every time of need.

Two or three days later a boy came from the same smallpox-infected district. By this time physicians in Michigan City had found out that the disease they had there was smallpox, and were going to put the house where he had been staying under quarantine. The brother who had just come thought he had sufficient faith to protect himself and others from the disease; but we who were older in the work and understood the ways of the Lord better, advised him to return, lest if he should have the smallpox in the city, they would put him in the pest-house, where he would not have the same chance to trust the Lord that he would if at home. So he returned to his home and had the disease there. Again God marvelously protected us.

A young sister came to the home for help in both soul and body. After earnest prayer in her behalf, we found that she was in no condition to get help to her soul until her body became stronger. She had greatly over-worked and her mind was about to give way. It was a month before we were able to talk to her at all about her soul. Her nerves were in such a condition that when she heard a prayer, a song, or a scripture, she could scarcely keep from screaming. As soon as she was able, we did all the Lord showed us to do for her soul. We found that all that God had laid to her charge was overworking and neglecting her spiritual life. Soon everything was made right with her soul, but it took months for her nerves and brain to get back to their normal condition.

We learned a good lesson from this incident. If we neglect our spiritual lives, we shall be losers every time. The Lord is a jealous God, and if he can't be first, he won't be second. If we want him to work in and through us, we must give him a chance to keep our souls replenished and ready for work. At different times while in city-work I have myself allowed temporal things to get too much on my mind, thus causing me to neglect my devotions. My spirituality would begin to weaken, and I would become less capable of being a blessing to souls. Had I been more diligent at certain times in secret prayer and searching the Scriptures, I should have been spared some sad experiences and heartaches.

One day the sister who was doing the cooking, made up a large batch of light bread, containing, I think, fifteen or twenty pounds of flour. The sister waited the proper length of time for the bread to rise, but it showed no signs at all of rising. Some of us talked the matter over and concluded that we could not afford to throw the flour away and that we had better ask God to make the bread rise. We did so, but the bread remained as lifeless as before. Finally a number of us gathered in the kitchen, knelt down on the floor, and asked God to make the bread rise. It was not long until our prayers were answered. That batch of dough made as good bread as I have ever eaten. God wonderfully stirred up the thanksgiving in our souls for this answer to prayer.

One of the company in the home had been exposed to the measles, and they were beginning to break out on his body. The Lord brought to his mind that he did not need to have the measles and that if he would put up a fight of faith against them, the Lord would heal him. He was anointed and prayed for, and God did put his rebuke on the affliction. The following day he exercised himself too much and had to have prayer again. That was on Saturday evening. Monday morning he was sufficiently well to start on a trip to Ohio to see his people. The possibilities of faith can not be comprehended by the finite mind of man. Well did the apostle say, "Faith is the substance of things hoped for, the evidence of things not seen."

Among many precious ones associated with us in the work in Chicago was Sister Clara Tuttle, now gone to her reward. She was a great help to my brother and me, and a blessing to the work in general. Shortly after she became acquainted with the truth, she asked the Lord what was her place in the body, and he told her it was to be a good mother. She filled her place well. This dear sister was not only a good mother to her own children, but to others, especially to the young workers who had no mother or whose mothers were unsaved. She not only gave good counsel to the young workers, but prayed with them in times of perplexity. Would to God there were more mothers in Israel like her! "Her children will rise up and call her blessed." I still remember the counsel she gave a brother who, was coming to the Missionary Home to stay for a time. "Now, brother, you have been acquainted with Brother Cole and his sister as gospel workers and have loved them dearly; but you have seen, them only in the pulpit and public meeting, where you have had but little opportunity to come in contact with their human weaknesses. When you go into the home to live with them, you will find that they are but human and make some mistakes. Be careful now that you do not judge them. Be careful that you don't allow these human weaknesses to hide the fact that they are ministers anointed by God to carry the gospel message to a lost world. Remember that God does not judge them from a human standpoint. If he judged any of us in that way, we should all be found wanting."

BIRTHDAY LINES

In Memory of February 5, 1822

Time moves on, and on, and onward, Piling up its teeming years; Each unfolds its store of blessings, Each one brings its joys and tears. Ninety years have thus been numbered Since one cold and wintry morn, On the fifth of February, When "our Mother Cole" was born.

While her little life was tender, Only in its babyhood, God removed her loving mother To a world more pure and good. Left now the little helpless baby Without mother's love or care, Many shadows o'er it hovered, Many sorrows it must share.

But her father kind and faithful Bro't much sunshine in her life; Tenderly he loved and blest her Until she became a wife. As a mother she was noble, Bore her lot with fortitude, Worried not o'er "sad tomorrows," But looked forward to the good.

When Life's cares and trials oppressed her, She had One in whom to trust; Lovingly He bore her sorrows, And in Him her soul was blest.

She had always words of kindness For the sad and those alone; And she often bore their sorrows As if they had been her own.

Old age does not foil the beauty Of her sweet unselfish ways; She still clings to Christ her Savior, On her lips are words of praise. Tho' upon her bed she lingers, There's no sorrow in her room, For her cheery words of comfort Dispel darkness and the gloom.

Like a sunbeam softly falling As if on an errand of love, Cheering up some lonely hour, Pointing to a world above; Or, the lily rich with fragrance, Shedding forth its sweet perfume, So the life of our dear mother Cheers and brightens up her room.

When her pilgrimage is ended, And her days are numbered here, She will only bloom the sweeter In that paradise o'er there. Soon the angels will be coming, Bear her to that land of rest, Where she'll ever be with Jesus, To rejoice among the blest.

Chapter XX

A Battle with Smallpox

Soon after we began work in the city, my brother George went out to assist in a meeting at Edgewood, Iowa. A mother desired prayer for her little girl, so my brother and another minister laid hands on her and prayed for her healing. The mother said that some one thought her child was taking smallpox, but that she was sure it was a mistake. The ministers saw a few little pimples on the child's lip and asked her if the same breaking-out was on other parts of her body. The mother's answer was, "None to speak of," and they reached the conclusion that the pimples on her lip were fever-sores. Under the impression that the child had nothing seriously wrong with her, my brother went to Roseville, Illinois, to begin a series of meetings. When the meeting had continued about a week, my brother began to be sick. Still in ignorance as to the nature of his sickness, he continued the meetings a few days longer. His illness increased and the first fever came upon him. The congregation was exposed before he knew what was the matter, but God overruled, answering the prayers of his children to protect all in attendance. When the nature of my brother's disease came to be fully understood, it seemed that all hopes of doing good at that place were blasted. Nevertheless, some seed had fallen on good ground, and these later brought forth precious fruit.

A sister who had been present at my brother's meetings, accepted the truth, got a good experience, and began living the life of a saint. Her nephew, Bro. John Murphy, now a minister of the church at Farmersville, California, came to visit her, bringing with him Bro. John Hauck. These two young men had been attending a Baptist college at Ottawa, Kans. A traveling minister who visited that place preached the doctrine of entire sanctification and these two young men sought and obtained the experience. The next morning after receiving the baptism of the Spirit, they started out like Abraham of old, not knowing whither they went, nor did they know where the Lord was leading them until they reached the home of Brother Murphy's aunt. Here they found a copy of *The Gospel Trumpet*.

As soon as they read *The Trumpet*, they knew where the Lord was leading them. They made their way to The Gospel Trumpet office, where Brother Murphy remained as a worker for two or three years and Brother Hauck for nearly ten years. Both are now ministers in this reformation. At least four ministers and four other workers at The Trumpet office, besides a score of other souls, have entered God's service through this sister's influence. So in spite of the fact that my brother thought that his labors at Roseville ended without results, many souls have been brought into the kingdom. "Cast thy bread upon the waters, and thou shalt find it after many days." "Drop a pebble in the water, just a splash and it is gone; but there are half a hundred ripples circling on, and on." "He that goeth forth and weepeth, bearing precious seed, shall doubtless come again with rejoicing bringing his sheaves with him."

My brother wrote me a card that he was not feeling well. On its receipt I was greatly burdened and felt led to go where he was, though I knew nothing about his condition. I waited until I received another message from him, which said that he was worse. I thought that God was leading me to go to him and felt a great burden as though I were going to meet something very serious, quite out of the ordinary. A number of other workers and I met and prayed for an hour before I went. I sent a telegram that I was coming. Some of the saints thought that I should wait until I got an answer to my telegram before starting; but I said, "No, God wanted me to telegraph that I was coming, and then start as quickly as possible." The Lord gave me this scripture: 1 Peter 4, commencing at the twelfth verse. The thirteenth verse was an especial comfort to me. I understood that I was going to meet something unusual, that I was going to have a severe battle in some way; but with this knowledge I had the admonition, "But rejoice, inasmuch as ye are partakers of Christ's sufferings." Two weeks before this God gave me the same scripture, with the impression that I should see its fulfilment in the near future.

I arrived at Roseville about twelve days after my brother had prayed for the little girl and found him already beginning to break out. We learned that the other minister who had been with him, took the disease about the same time. For a day or two after my arrival, however, we were not certain that my brother had the smallpox. As soon as we were convinced of the nature of the disease, we sent for a physician to come and quarantine us so that others would be protected, and the battle began.

The doctor called every day, said he had to come to protect the home where we were staying. He vaccinated quite a number, including me and Sister Elizabeth Hill, who was helping me care for brother George. Sister Hill trusted the Lord that the vaccination would not take. Her faith proved effectual. I thought I had to let the vaccination take, did not resist, and so had a severe time of it. I was the sickest when my brother needed the greatest attention - just as the scales were falling off.

The doctor did his best to get a chance to treat my brother. He worked by strategy and seemed to have some new scheme every day. He shut me out of the room and tried to force my brother to take medicine when he was too weak to think. He made my brother promise to use the medicine and then tried to make me promise that I would see that it was used. I told him I would do as my brother said. After the doctor's departure, I had a little talk with George, and he decided to continue trusting the Lord.

From the very beginning he had put his case in God's hands. When the fever reached its height and the disease was at its climax, God rebuked it, and soon my brother was on the road to recovery. Inside of an hour the fever was going down and in twelve hours it was entirely gone. The same evening the fever was rebuked, the doctor came. My brother said, "Doctor, I am better." "Yes," he answered, "But not permanently so." "Yes," said my brother, "permanently, and I know where the healing came from. God sent it, and I know I shall not get worse." From that time forward his improvement was rapid.

Soon after that the effects of the disease settled in his

eyes, and for a time it seemed that his sight would be destroyed, but in answer to prayer his eyes began to recover and were soon all right again. Then the pox attacked his nose, closing the nostrils so that it seemed almost to kill him to breathe. It was during one of these times that the doctor was most determined to push his remedies on him, and he succeeded, too, in a small measure. The medicine was applied once or twice, but God made it very clear to me that he had the case in his own hands, and we applied ourselves to prayer. In less than an hour the obstructions were removed from his nose, and he breathed like a little child, so easily that we could scarcely hear his breath across the room.

Then came the doctor's last attempt to push remedies on us. He said we needed something to keep his face from pitting, declaring that unless some remedies were used it would pit badly. Again we sought the Lord in prayer. There was but one pit left on his face, and that would not be noticed unless attention were called to it. God proved the doctor wrong in every point by not leaving a trace of the disease on my brother's body.

After the fever went down, it was with difficulty that my brother was kept warm. It was late in the fall, the weather was cold, and my brother's blood was so thin it would have been very easy for him to take cold. The doctor carried out smallpox laws to the extreme, putting up a wet sheet in my brother's door as he was scaling off. I felt rather bold: as said of one of old, I wasn't afraid of the king's command. So at night I put the wet sheet back so that my brother could get the warmth of the fire. In the morning I put the sheet back across the door before the doctor came.

But we had not fought this battle through alone. His

church in general were praying earnestly for us. It seemed when we plead the promises we touched an agreement, and it was like a mighty cable. We felt so secure and were so hedged in by prayer and faith that when I thought of the danger of taking the smallpox, it seemed I could exercise faith so easily in agreement. It was very easy for me to say, "By faith I know God will not let me take it." After I was vaccinated, some one said to me, "Now you feel more safe, don't you?" My answer was "No, I have no confidence in that at all. My confidence is in the Lord. It is he who has protected me. He shall have all the glory."

What few letters we had a chance to write, had to be dictated to some one standing about thirty yards away from us. During this time I concluded that if ever there was a disease followed by the persecutions of the devil, it was the smallpox. Before this I had sometimes thought that Job's affliction was the small pox, but I now came to the conclusion that I was mistaken. Had his disease been smallpox, his three comforters would not have hung around him as they did to torture him.

The enemy tried to inflict punishment upon us in every way he could. A great many in the neighborhood felt hurt because George had unconsciously brought the disease to that part of the country. Then the doctor, besides trying to push his remedies upon us and to make us as uncomfortable as possible in trusting the Lord, created all the sentiment he could against us in the neighborhood. At the same time he was making all the money he could by vaccinating others. One woman that was vaccinated at that time, had varioloid, so the doctor said. The county built a pest-house for her and her husband. This, together with his other charges, cost the county eight hundred dollars. This woman, so I was informed, thought she was immune from the disease and when smallpox broke out the next fall, undertook to nurse those who were having it. Again the doctor's words were proved false. She took the smallpox and died. It will always do to trust God; man is weak at best.

When George was about to recover, the authorities wanted to raise the quarantine too soon, thus exposing others to danger. Defeated in this attempt, their next move was to hold us longer than necessary. I had been praying that if the enemy tried to work in either way, God would defeat their purpose.

I am sure it would have done your soul good to hear my brother when he had recovered sufficiently to get up and walk around. He walked the floor singing this song:

"How can you part with Jesus,
So loving, so kind and gracious!
His service to me is precious;
I am happy as I can be.

I love my Lord; He loveth me.
The life of a Christian suits me;
I am happy as I can be."

He would sing the song over and over and then praise God. It was good of the Lord to so wonderfully sustain and protect him and all of us through this affliction.

I do not know that any of us are able to appreciate as we should even the prayers of the saints during this trying time; not to speak of the generous offers of help made by some of the dear ones in the Lord and the unsaved members of my own family.

One of my unsaved brothers and a sister minister, both having families, volunteered to come and help me care for George if I needed them. But I felt that to accept their offer would endanger their families unnecessarily, and told them that the Lord would help us and that we would get along. It touched our hearts, however, to think that they would risk their lives for our help and comfort. We appreciated all this to the extent of our abilities, and our hearts were melted in real thanksgiving because of such kindness.

Every now and then during the quarantine I would get real hungry for encouragement and consolation. At such times my prayer was, "O Lord, give me some scripture that will be a help to me." The Lord would invariably point me to 1 Peter 4:12 and 13, laying emphasis especially on the thirteenth verse. The Lord showed me that he wanted me to rejoice more. I would reply: "Lord, I thought I got out of that scripture all there was in it. I thought I had rejoiced all I could." At such times his answer would be, "You can rejoice more; there is more in it for you yet." Like a good teacher, he held me to the lesson until I learned it well.

When we are in affliction, remember there is some lesson in it for us which we must learn. If we do not get it, the Lord will have to repeat the experience - give us the lesson over - because it was not learned the first time. By learning the lesson thoroughly the first time, we avoid its repetition.

I remember a prayer that was much on my lips during this trial of which I have been speaking: "Lord, help me to get out of the fire what you have in it for me, and help me to leave in the fire what you want me to be rid of." Even with the preparation this trial gave me, I was none too well prepared to encounter some things I had to meet soon afterward. God knew his business. He knew what was coming, knew the lesson I needed and gave it to me at the proper time. It pays to be submissive to God. If we are fully submitted into his hands, he will prepare us by the proper schooling for every test of life and in every difficulty bring us off more than conquerors.

While my brother's illness was so severe, we were so wonderfully held up by the prayers of God's children that we did not feel the weight of the affliction that we were passing through. When my brother was sufficiently recovered, however, that the church got the news that he was getting better, their prayers were not so constant. By that time the sister at whose home I was staying and who had assisted me so faithfully in caring for my brother, was almost overcome by the long strain she had undergone. In fact, we were both almost ready to collapse. In our weak condition we felt the need of the prayers of others, but as the church had the impression that my brother was so far recovered that he no longer needed help, we had to fight the battle alone. I learned this, that no matter how much others help us by their prayers in time of trial, when we become able to take on responsibility ourselves, God requires us to do all we can for our own help and protection. It was at this time that I felt very keenly that I should have rejoiced more when the trial was on.

Chapter XXI

Camp-Meetings in Various States

While engaged in the work in Chicago I had the privilege of attending camp-meetings in a number of States. While at a camp-meeting at Grand Forks, N. Dakota, I received an invitation to attend a meeting at Hammond, Louisiana, about 1,500 miles south. For some time I had had a desire to go to that part of the country for different reasons, and therefore gladly embraced this opportunity. I went by way of Chicago, remaining at the home for about a week.

The kindness of my reception in the South gave me the impression that people in the South are very hospitable and large-hearted. I think that in this respect they excel many of our Northern and Eastern people. I found that in the South much is expected of ministers coming from the East or the North. The responsibilities of the meeting, therefore, were all that I could go through, even with the help of the Lord. It was July, and the weather was so warm that we could not use the tabernacle during the heat of the day, but had to resort to a little grove near by.

During this meeting I went twelve miles and visited my brother's grave; on this trip I also called on some saints who lived in that part of the country. I had a pleasant drive and also got a chance to enjoy some of the Southern figs which grow in those parts. Notwithstanding I was much fatigued when I returned that evening and thought I would not go out to meeting at all. Then I thought I would go for the first of the service and return to my lodging before the meeting closed, as I would be too tired to remain. But God planned otherwise. He showed me that I must trust him for strength and be prepared to preach that evening. God delivered the message through me and blessed it to the salvation of a number of souls.

Soon after the camp-meeting I returned to Chicago. As I started homeward, I found that the oppressive heat had greatly reduced my strength. Because of the heat, too, I had been tempted to drink too much ice-water, lemonade, etc. When about sixty miles from home, my heart began to fail, and I saw that unless the Lord helped me I was not going to be able to get through. I can not express to you how earnestly I called upon God. Almost every moment of the time from there on I trusted the Lord to hold me up, for it seemed that in spite of myself my heart would fail. The Lord came to my rescue. I reached my destination all right, and suffered no serious harm later.

One fall I went to the camp-meeting at Carthage, Mo. At this meeting I met some of my old friends from Maries County, Missouri, and other places, some of whom I had not met for more than twenty years. One of them was a brother whom I first met near Rolla, Mo. Seeing him reminded me of an incident that occurred in connection with his mother-in-law, old Sister Bell, at the time I was holding meetings in that part of the country. She was a large woman. One winter she slipped on the ice and came near breaking her back.

The accident occurred in the middle of the week, and until the following Sunday morning she was paralyzed.

The meeting that Sunday was at the Bell home. We found her lying helpless. As we talked to her about her healing, she seemed anxious to be healed. She was a good, pure saint, and lived close to the Lord. In the prayer before preaching we were especially burdened for her and prayed earnestly that God would heal her. God encouraged our hearts. After preaching we again talked to her a little while and quoted some of the promises. I told her how God had heard and answered prayer for my healing; I had had an attack of some disease a day or two before, and God had wonderfully delivered me from it. As we talked, her faith seemed to grow by bounds and leaps. We asked her if she was willing to die. She said she was; and again, if she was willing to live if the Lord wanted her to, and again she answered yes. Then we asked her if she believed the Lord would heal her. She said she did. Her husband and oldest daughter were standing by, expecting her to die any minute. Her mother, who was a skeptic, was also present. She wanted me to persuade her daughter to take medicine. I replied that I would talk to her daughter, but did not tell her what I would say.

When I found out that the sister's faith was strong in God, I did what I could to encourage her to trust God for immediate healing. All at once, while we were talking, she said, "The Lord heals me." Her husband, fearing that the death-struggle was coming on, went to hold her in bed. I told him to let her go - that this was of God and that he would take care of her. She bounded out of bed and went running through the house, saying that God had healed her and that a sluice of praise was going through her soul. Her son-in-law was not present, so I hastened over to his house to tell him the good news. "Do you know what came to me first?" said he. "No," I answered. "Well, it came to me that she was lying in bed all this time to have a chance to show off on Sunday, but I know she isn't a hypocrite, and therefore it isn't that way. But I am glad I wasn't there, for fear I should have had to believe." When I met this brother at Carthage, Missouri, he was not, I am sorry to say, as strong in the faith as was his privilege. He had made great improvement, however. How cruel is unbelief! It makes God a liar and causes one to believe the devil.

From Carthage I went to Webb City, Missouri, where I visited friends and saints whom I had known years before. Among the number was mother Sunderland. [Footnote: Since the above statement was written, Mother Sunderland has gone to her reward.] From Webb City I went to Chanute,

Kansas, and visited two saints, old friends of mine who needed encouragement. While at Chanute I ate something that did not agree with me. I partly recovered, and then went on to Neosho Falls, Kansas, where I remained for two weeks and held a few services. As I still had severe sick spells, I sent for prayers to The Trumpet office and the saints in Kansas City and Chicago. The sister with whom I was staying held on to God, pleading the promises in my behalf like a hero, and with such importuning faith that I was soon able to pursue my journey.

I made my next stop at Kansas City, remaining there for nearly a month, I think. When I first arrived at that place, I was quite weak. I did not fully comprehend how sick I had been. Bro. James Peterman, who had charge of the home, was called away the first Sunday after I arrived, and so I had charge of both services. I walked three-quarters of a mile three times that day and preached twice. The next day I walked a mile and a half, most of the way up hill. My exertions proved entirely too much for me, and I endured some rather severe suffering. My body was badly worn out, and as a result my mind got into a sad, discouraged mood. My meditations were something like this: I shall soon be getting old and helpless, and not able to do much in the work. If I live, it will not be long until I shall be a burden upon some one else.

It was a late hour before my nerves got sufficiently quieted so that I could rest. The next morning I had a dream. I saw a little child about two years old playing on the floor. Some one came by and stepped on the little one's fingers, and it began to cry with pain. His father came along, took him up in his arms and caressed him, and very soon the pain was all gone, and the little fellow was all right again. It seemed that the father had such love and pity for the child that I felt the effects of it in my own soul. When I awoke I said, "Lord, what is there in this dream for me?" I realized that no doubt God had permitted it for my good. Immediately this scripture came to me: "Like as a father pitieth his children, so the Lord pitieth them that fear him." The Lord seemed to say to my soul, "Now I want to pity you." I accepted his kindness as best I knew how.

I thought I had gotten out of the dream all the benefit that the Lord had in it for me; but when I went to rise and dress myself, God spoke again, saying, "Don't be in a hurry. I want to have a chance to pity you." Then he kept bringing to my mind his goodness in a way that touched the right spot, covered my need, and at last I was permitted to arise and dress. After I was dressed the following words came to me: "He knoweth our frame; he remembereth that we are but dust." The dream was still so visible before me. I could still see the father pitying his child, and I felt the strength of that pity in my own soul. It was so real that I comprehended as I never had before in my life, something of the depths of God's pity for his children. Had it been some person dealing with me, he might have said, "Oh, you didn't need to let the cloud come over you. You didn't need to have the blues in this way." But instead of speaking to me in that manner, God just poured out his pity until he chased all the dark clouds away, until his presence filled the vacancy, until he satisfied every longing of my soul.

Dear ones, we have a merciful high priest, who is touched with the feeling of our infirmities, who was in all points tempted like as we are, yet without sin. Therefore he is able to succor them that are tempted. Do you not think he will do to trust? Then, let us trust him and not be afraid, though the clouds seem dark and lowering. God will do to trust in the storms and tempests of life the same as when it is calm - only during the storm he will have a better chance to reveal his mercy, his goodness, and his power.

After being with the dear ones in the Kansas City home for nearly a month, I returned to Chicago. Upon my arrival in the city I found that my body was quite run down. Yet God enabled me to do quite active service. No doubt, however, I went at times when, if I had consulted the Lord more carefully, he would have said rest. I was not able to be nearly so active as I had been in the past, and God seemed directing me to take a change, as city-work means constant activity. About a year after my former visit, I again went to Kansas City to visit the work there for a season, remaining there for about three months. I enjoyed the work there very much, although I could take on but little responsibility. God blessed my efforts.

In Kansas City I saw in operation the method of working through the circulating library and cottage-meetings. They had quite a number of the different books printed at The Trumpet office. These are loaned in various parts of the city by the workers from the home, who visit the homes, talk with the readers, take up the books that have already been read, and loan new ones. The reading of the books often opens the way for cottage-meetings, which are held by the workers and young ministers from the home. The holding of these meetings serve two purposes; namely, getting the truth to the people and affording an opportunity to the young ministers and workers to get experience in gospel work.

After being in Kansas City a time, I went to see some old friends at Kingston, Mo. God led us to have two or three services a week for about two weeks. After about two weeks two of the sisters from the missionary home in Kansas City were sent for, and we had a two weeks' meeting.

While I was at Kingston, God in different ways gave me much needed encouragement. One day a sister was giving her adopted daughter some good advice on the subject of marriage. Among other things, the sister told the girl that if she married in God's order she would have some one to love her and care for her in her old age. The enemy took advantage of this to hurl a dart at me, because I was growing old, might soon become helpless, and had no one to sympathize with or care for me. For a time everything seemed dark, as though God had let me see certain things and had then veiled his face from me. I wondered why this was. I meditated: "Well, I have obeyed the Lord, have done what he wanted me to do. He certainly will not forsake me now. If I should live to be old and helpless, he will not let any serious thing come on me, because I have been obedient."

About this time God spoke to my soul, calling my attention to the thirty-seventh Psalm, third and fourth verses: "Trust in the Lord, and do good." Now, this was my part. This is what God required of me - to trust in him and do good. Then came his part: "So shall thou dwell in the land, and verily thou shalt be fed." His part was to see that I had a place to stay and sufficient food. The scriptures that he brought to my mind at that time have not lost their sweetness and power even to this day.

I can not tell you how precious these special lessons of God have been to me; how they have helped my feet to press the everlasting rock, He is a covenant-keeping God, and his Word is true and forever settled in heaven. Well might the Psalmist say, "I have been young, and now am old; yet have I not seen the righteous forsaken, nor his seed begging bread. He is ever merciful, and lendeth; and his seed is blessed." Never again has the enemy dared to tempt me in this way.

Praise the Lord! Truly he is all that we take him for by faith. "All things are yours." "Ye are Christ's, and Christ is God's." Will he not with him freely give you all things? The Father gave the Son, heaven's best gift, and did he leave out the minor gifts? Nay, verily, he will fulfil every promise to the letter if we meet the conditions. It was Joshua who said, I think, "Not one of these good promises has failed." Neither have any of them failed any of us who put our trust in Him. Heaven and earth shall pass away, but his word will stand secure. "Forever, O Lord, thy word is settled in heaven."

"Even down to old age, all my people shall prove,
My sovereign, eternal, unchangeable love;
And when hoary hairs shall their temples adorn,
They'll still like lambs in my bosom be borne."

After being in Kingston one month, we came to Kansas City, remained a short time, made a call some distance out to pray for the sick, and on my return to the city had urgent word to come to Chicago, as my mother was needing my attention. After a short stay in Chicago I went to the camp-meeting at Anderson, Indiana, and enjoyed the feast there. Then I went out in the country near Summitville, Indiana, for a little rest and recreation. I was at Summitville about five weeks and during that time assisted Bro. N. S. Duncan in a series of meetings that God blessed and owned.

Shortly after this I felt led to go to Iowa a few weeks to be what help I could to a dear sister who was going through some deep trials. Her difficulty seemed to be mainly self-accusation. In other words, she had set her spiritual standard so high that she could not live up to her own ideal. Like nearly all people who undergo that difficulty, she was good at heart, but the struggle to get out of her difficulty was severe. God came to her help, gave her victory over her trials, such as she had never been able to have before. She has never been troubled again in the same manner, and she is now firmly established in the way of the Lord.

Some of God's dear little ones who are very conscientious, sometimes look upon the Lord as a severe father. It seems to them that he, like Pharaoh, wants them to make brick without straw, to gather stubble. With this idea of God in mind, they have a hard time and fail to see him as a good, kind, loving heavenly Father, one whose heart is overflowing with mercy and compassion for his dear tried children, ready to make a way for their escape. In fact, if they could but see it, he has already made a way of escape and wants to help them into it just as soon as they will let him. His promises cover the need of every one. If taken and belived, one promise of itself is sufficient. "God is faithful, who will not suffer you to be tempted above that ye are able to bear; but will with the temptation also make a way to escape, that ye may be able to bear it."

While the fire is hottest, let us stop and think that this kind Father will not permit the flames to be any severer or the fire any hotter than is most for our good, and that he has a bright design in all that he permits to come upon us. He wants us to hold still, so that he can bring out his design in us. Let us be careful that we do not foil his plans. If we do not, not only will he be pleased, but we also shall be glad that we submitted to him.

I spent five weeks laboring with this sister. Perhaps some will think that a long time to spend on one soul, and even think the time wasted, but did you ever think how great is the value God places upon one soul? "For what shall it profit a man, if he shall gain the whole world, and lose his own soul? Or what shall a man give in exchange for his soul?" According to the Lord's estimate, one soul is worth more than the whole world. Nor do we know how many other souls that one will bring to the Lord - like the one woman at the well to whom Jesus delivered a message and who went and told many others. Let us be faithful, therefore, in helping souls, whether it be one or many.

Chapter XXII

Caring for my Aged Mother

Provision had now been made for the removal of my mother to the Old People's Home at Anderson, Ind. As there was not sufficient help at the home then to care for her, I took that duty upon myself. As soon as help should come, I was to be free to go and be in meetings what little I was able, except when I needed to care for her, either when she was sick or when they were short of help.

In the days following my coming to Anderson, I went to Sioux Falls, S. Dakota, to visit a sister who was needing some special encouragement. It was mid-winter. Some told me before I started that there was danger of my being snow-bound, and advised me to take plenty of provisions with me; but as I did not anticipate any such difficulty, I did not heed the warning. We got along pretty well until about ten miles from Sioux Falls. The recent heavy snows had so obstructed the way that the engine could not pull through. It would run a little way into the drift, then back up, and again push its way into the drift as far as possible. It kept working its way forward in this manner from one o'clock in the afternoon until very nearly midnight, when we arrived at Sioux Falls.

Mary Cole

Sure enough, my provisions did run out on the way; but with the generosity peculiar to most people under like circumstances, the other passengers, although strangers to me, helped me out and supplied all the food needed. Doubtless many of these people knew nothing of real salvation, but their liberal-heartedness proved that sin had not effaced all of the marks of God's love from their hearts.

I remained six weeks at Sioux Falls, during which time I had but little chance to do missionary work other than to encourage the sister whom I went to visit. However, I did go out and put Trumpets in some of the yards and on the porches of neighboring houses. Possibly some of these papers may have proved silent messengers of salvation. Sometimes when the mercury was ten degrees below zero, and the snow deep on the ground, I would go out and walk and distribute Trumpets or tracts. In spite of the cold and snow, I enjoyed my stay. I did what God directed me to do, and I trust that he has blessed my labors. At any rate, the sister whom I went to visit has written me a number of times that she does not know what she would have done had not God sent me at that time to help her through the difficulties she was then encountering. On my return trip I took a severe cold while traveling in a chilly car. My train was late and did not make connections at Chicago. I telephoned out to the Faith Missionary Home, and they gave me an invitation to come and remain over night. I accepted their kindness and was soon in the home where I had spent so many years in the work of the Lord. That evening I made a call on a dear sister that I was anxious to meet, and by the time I got back to the home again I was real sick. I had taken a severe attack of the grip and was suffering greatly. Most of the workers were gone to meetings in different parts of the city, but a sister who had remained at home, laid her hands on me and prayed the prayer of faith. I was able next morning to resume my journey back to the Old People's Home at Anderson.

Although my system had been greatly weakened and rendered more liable to taking cold than it had been before, yet I was well enough so that I soon went about fifteen miles to the little town of Cammack and assisted Sister Maud Smith in a two weeks' meeting. Soon after my return I took a severe attack of pneumonia. Prayer was offered, but the disease seemed to be stubborn. I was anointed, and prayer was again offered, but the battle was still on. So we called in some more of God's ministers and again had prayer. This time God healed me, and next day I was able to go down to dinner. Nevertheless, I remained weak for some days, but soon felt almost entirely restored to health.

In about two weeks, however, I took another attack of pneumonia, one more severe than the first. Again we had a stubborn fight. We prayed three times before any effects were visible. Pleurisy was setting in, and I had begun to spit blood. My temperature had reached 103-3/4 when God gave the witness from heaven that he healed me. I did not get strength nearly so quickly as I did before, and had to keep my bed most of the time for two days. Nevertheless, I never doubted once my healing, and indeed it had been accomplished. I have never suffered from that affliction since.

This is only one of the many times that the Lord has come to my rescue and touched my body. Sometimes I have been healed instantly, and at other times God has given me the witness that I was healed, but my strength returned gradually and it was several days before I could be about as usual. However, the healing came. God was doing the work in his own way, and he always has a purpose and reason for any method he may use. Let us not question the method he uses, but trust him.

Since coming to the Old People's Home I have not been privileged to go out much to help in meetings. This has been partly due to the fact that Mother has needed much care and also to the fact that my strength has not been equal to the exertion. But I have had the privilege of helping in other ways. Very often the old people in the home need prayer for their healing or help and encouragement in their souls. Besides, I have had the privilege of giving help and encouragement to some of the workers in The Trumpet office, and also to others living nearby. I am very thankful for these opportunities.

The Lord has also been helping me to trust him for means to support his cause in the Missionary field and other places. Although I can not give much, yet I appreciate the privilege of giving the little. At first I felt led to purpose forty cents a month. The Lord provided this sum every time. For a year I kept up this purpose and never once had to borrow. The Lord also provided means for me to help his cause in other directions. The next year I felt led to ask God to help me trust him for fifty cents a month for missionary work. I never failed to have my money ready at the proper time. The third year I felt like trusting the Lord for seventy-five cents a month, paying this amount in advance. One consideration that made me reach the decision to pay in advance was that if God should call me before the month was out I should not be in debt. I have never been disappointed. Sometimes the Lord gives me happy surprises in this as well as in other things. If we give God a chance, he will develop our faith to trust him for means as well as for other things, if we are not able to work and earn the money, and have a desire to help his cause. During the present year in which I am writing, I am trusting the Lord for a dollar a month for foreign missionary work, and early in the spring the Lord gave me enough to pay my purpose for the whole year. He made it clear to me that I should use the money for that purpose.

The Lord has helped me also to trust him for my clothing and other needs, and for the needs of my mother. He is such a present help. A number of times I have asked him for money in the morning, and before the sun went down I had all that I asked for. "According to your faith," says the Word, "so be it unto thee." "The desire of the righteous shall be granted."

Some persons have thought that God did not answer prayer for the healing of old people, since they would soon have to die anyway. We know that God will not make them young again, as that is not his plan; but since coming to the Old People's Home I have witnessed the healing of many aged people. In fact, my mother, the oldest inmate of the home, has trusted God for a number of years. The older she gets, the stronger her faith seems to be. Every time these old people are afflicted, the Lord answers prayer. In asking God for healing, they seem childlike, and simple, fully expect God to heal them when they call upon him.

One of the inmates of the home, an old lady in her eighty-seventh year was at the point of death. From appearances one would have supposed that her end was near. She had no hope of recovery. Her burial clothes were made ready. She had been prayed for a number of times, but was still suffering great agony. She did not know what was causing the suffering, but thought it might be appendicitis. Some of us, however, could not be satisfied to let her die without making further effort for her healing, so we sent for Bro. E. E. Byrum. She was again anointed and prayed for. While we were on our knees, God assured my heart that he would hear and answer prayer. Her suffering did not seem to decrease, however, immediately, and in less than an hour Brother Byrum was again called. He came at once, as he had remained in the house. The second time he offered prayer that God would relieve her of her suffering. Although her condition still looked discouraging, yet God made us know that she was going to get well. Although she did not recover very rapidly, yet for one of her age the change was marvelous, and not long afterward she had her usual health. A year or more afterwards she was able to return to Pennsylvania to visit some of her folks. She concluded to remain there and is still living in that State.

One of the aged brothers in the home was greatly afflicted. His mind was giving way somewhat, and he got into a very melancholy condition, thinking that he ought never to leave his room, and especially that he should not be out-of-doors. It could easily be seen that if he continued very long in this condition, he would not only lose his mind but be bedfast and perhaps die. He desired very much to be sanctified and asked several of us to come to his room and pray for him. We went to his room and talked to him on the subject of sanctification, and while he was surrendering all to the

Lord, we had him consecrate his will that he would be out-of-doors all that the Lord wanted him to be. He promised he would do so, and the Lord sanctified him. In the two years or more that have passed since then, he has not broken his promise, but has remained in the house only when the weather prevented his being out. As a result, his mind is almost entirely restored, his body is much stronger, and he is not like the same person.

In the four years I have been in the Old People's Home nursing my mother, I have noticed that the older people get the less able they are to comprehend anything new. For this reason it is hard for an old person to grasp the promises of God for salvation; but if they have been saved in their younger years and have lived a consistent Christian before they come to such a great age, they will every year grow more and more like Jesus, trusting him more fully, and seem more humble and thankful as they draw nearer the grave. I have been more strongly impressed than ever before that people should seek God while they are young before they become unable to grasp the promises. I feel the more impressed to sound a warning because there are some in the home with whom we have labored again and again, but who are so aged and infirm that seemingly they can not reach a decision to seek until they find. Their unsaved condition, in view of their extreme age, puts them in a very serious place.

The spiritual workers in The Trumpet Family sometimes take me with them to visit those who need help in the city. One day we went to see a man who was on his death-bed. He had never known God. When we first went into the room, we did not know that he would be able to talk with us much, but we prayed earnestly that God's Spirit would work with him. That was all we could do at that time. Later we went and had prayer with him again, talking to him about his soul, and prayed earnestly that God would spare his life until he could obtain salvation, and that God would keep his mind clear so that he would be able to meet the conditions. We went to see him the third time. In the meantime other workers had been to see him, and he was becoming concerned about his soul. While one of the brethren was praying with him, he grasped the promises that God would save him, and was able to rejoice in the Lord. When I went to see him a little later, he seemed to have complete victory and was very happy.

While thinking of this occurrence at a later time, it seemed to me that I had done nothing toward the brother's salvation, since I was not present at the time he was saved. But the Lord began to talk to my soul: "Paul may plant, and Apollos may water, but God gives the increase. Are you not willing to plant and let some one else water? Are you not willing to be coworkers with others for the Lord?" I saw the point and answered, "Amen, Lord, I am willing; any way to get souls saved."

One day my mother was taken suddenly ill. Her affliction was overflowing of the gall. It seemed that she would strangle to death. She was anointed and prayer was offered; then we sent for the elders and again had prayer, but it seemed that she was dying. A few hours later, thinking she was dying, we sent for some of the elders and a number of us gathered about her bed. The blood seemed to be settling under her skin as though she were mortifying before she died, and the Superintendent, who was standing near the bed, said he was sure he heard the death-rattle in her throat. Even at that time we offered prayer the third time, and all these more pronounced symptoms disappeared and she looked natural once more. She remained quite sick, however, for several days. God had made it clear to one of the brethren that we had offered the prayer of faith and that her life would be spared for a time. She is still living at this time, a marvel of God's divine power.

Chapter XXIII

Exhortation to Workers and Ministers

In conclusion I feel that the Lord would be pleased for me to say a few words for the encouragement of young ministers and workers. In my work in the ministry I have come through many varied experiences that, I trust, will be helpful to you in the trials through which you will have to pass before you get settled in the Lord's work.

The first difficulty met by most young ministers and workers is in regard to their call. Unless the call be clear and definite, they are likely to be in some doubt as to whether or not they are called, and thus be exposed to the temptations of the enemy that God has not called them at all. Sometimes God makes a call so clear that it is beyond question, and the one called has no chance to doubt it for a moment. This was my experience at first; but when I got my mind filled with other plans, instead of keeping in view the past leadings of the Lord, sad to say, I began to doubt my call. But when I began again to seek God's will, everything cleared up, and I felt certain of my call.

Many others have difficulties right on this point. They feel led to do something for the Lord, and undertake to follow the leadings of his Spirit, but they do not feel the presence of God as they expected to feel it, or do not have the liberty that they think they should have. Then comes the temptation, "Has God called me, or am I trying to push out without any calling?" If they are very conscientious, it is easy for them to become confused when confronted with this temptation. They will pray over it and trouble over it. They are very timid and feel afraid to ask older workers lest what they have supposed to be a call is an imagination of their own and they will get a good sharp rebuke. They will struggle along in this condition until it becomes unbearable; then perhaps they will open their hearts to some person in whom they have confidence. If they get the proper instruction, they can soon be lifted out of this dilemma; but if not, they may do as some have done before - get so confused that they will lose the grace of God out of their souls.

My advice would be: If you have any idea that you are called, go to exercising yourself as best you can, whether it be in exhortation, teaching, or testimony, or whatever God brings most clearly to your mind. If you are not sure about your calling, in the meantime be patient and wait on God. Be sure you cast your burden entirely on him and let him bear it for you. If God's hand is on you for service, you will sooner or later be perfectly satisfied as to what he wants you to do; but if it should be otherwise, and you are honest of heart, you will be only too glad to know that you are not called. Thus your mind will be relieved.

If you are exercising yourself in spiritual things and no one is getting any benefit, you should take time to consider well whether God is calling you or not. I verily believe that if God's hand is on any one for service, whether he be a beginner or some one of experience, some will get a blessing when he teaches, exhorts, or delivers a message, because with his Word, God gives the anointing of his Spirit. "But the manifestation of the Spirit is given to every man to profit withal" (1 Corinthians 12:7). According to the Word, then, we can safely say that if there is no profit to the hearers in what is being set forth, God's Spirit is not inditing the message.

A young worker who was doubtful about his call, once went to an older brother for advice. This is what he received: "If you feel that God wants you to go out into evangelistic work, go right along, even if you are not sure that God is calling you. Go along, and then if you have success, you will know it is your own efforts and trust in God that has brought success, and not the efforts and faith of another. By following this plan you can easily determine whether or not God's hand is on you for the work."

Now, the method the brother proposed might succeed in some cases all right, but I hardly think it would do in all cases, as all are not led out alike. One of my brothers, when he was first called, felt led to be with me in the work, that God might make me more useful by his presence. He did not comprehend at all that God's hand was on him for service, but later God began to lead him out and to use and bless his efforts. By and by God got him to the point where he could reveal to him his future work. At first my brother hardly knew what to do. He was at a place where he had to fulfil his calling or else grieve God. He chose the former course, and God made him a useful minister, but his development was gradual.

If you begin exercising yourself in the ministry, and

God does not bless your efforts, and God's children do not realize that his Spirit is working through you, you would do well to go slowly and to keep submitted to the brethren, lest you should find yourself running ahead of the leadings of the Spirit of the Lord. If God is leading a young worker out for service, he not only will make him feel sooner or later the weight of the call, but will so impress the church that they will know that God is inditing his message.

When you once get it definitely settled that you are called to the ministry, never allow the difficulties and trials of this life so to cloud your vision that you doubt your call. It is one of the tricks of the enemy by trials and discouragement to make the ministers doubt their calling. When your call is once settled, do not go over it again and again to find out whether God is in earnest about it. If you should backslide, of course, then you should wait until God makes clear his will to you again. If a person is not stable in his experience, even though he has had a call to service, that call does not remain so clear and God does not always trust him at once after his recovery from his unsettled state.

Some young workers who feel clear that God has called them to service, try to measure their call by what others think of it. Such a course will bring on confusion. It is all right to be submissive to the brethren, but the Lord wants each of us to get his own bearings. Pray through until you get the mind of God, and at the same time be subordinate to the brethren. If they see it is not best for you to move out rapidly, heed what they tell you.

Be sure to keep your own individuality. If you feel that God has shown you a duty, do it in his fear, in a humble, submissive way. God may be leading you, and yet he may not be making his design very clear to others. There may be many difficulties in your way, such as bashfulness, want of fluent speech, awkwardness of manner, and ignorance. If, however, God has called you, and you keep submissive to him, he will in his own way bring out his design in you. Whatever your hands find to do, do it with your might. One has said, "Instant obedience is the secret of divine guidance."

Some young workers become discouraged if they are not used extensively. You need not conclude, however, that because the Lord does not give you a message often, he does not want to use you at all. Keep submitted and obey God. If God is leading you into evangelistic work, move out. If many souls are saved, be thankful; but if few are saved, still be thankful. Obey God. Do all that he shows you to do, and expect souls to be saved. Pray earnestly that God may convict souls. Pray through until you know that God is going to work with you for the salvation of mankind. Be so true, so humble, and so faithful, and so fill your calling by the help of God, that you can say with Paul, "I magnify mine office."

During my evangelistic labors I have come to places where from a natural standpoint the prospect was so discouraging and the religious confusion of the people so great that, if we could not have interceded with God for help, it would have been useless for us to remain. When we went to God in earnest prayer, however, and plead with him for souls, God never disappointed us. Many times we have had our greatest victories where the prospects seemed especially discouraging.

As we have already said, a definite call is the first essential for a gospel worker; but even with such a call a minister will fail, unless he goes forth filled with the Spirit. You may have a call, you may really be sent by the Lord; but unless you keep filied with the Spirit, your labors will soon cease to bring results. Do not try to imitate the manner and methods of others, but keep yourself so submitted to God and so pliable in his hands that he can have his way with you, even as the potter does with the clay.

Let God mold and fashion you into a vessel after his own design.

Again, do not neglect to search the Scriptures. Under the illumination of the Holy Spirit, the Scriptures will prove a mine of wealth to you. Education is all right in its place; but when you lean upon it as a means of understanding the Scriptures, or when you depend upon it for unction and liberty and for ability to teach, preach, or exhort, you will make a sad failure. You will disappoint yourself, the people, and God.

Do not question your calling because you have a poor education. Make good use of your present opportunities. Read good books. Get all the help and information you can in regard to soul-saving, but be careful you do not lean on your education for soul-unction. Many a time the Lord has called my attention to this thought before I rose to address an audience. Again and again he has reminded me to be sure not to depend upon myself, but to lean always on him, to drink in of his Spirit, so that I might give out to others. Human speech fails me in trying to bring out the importance of this thought. I trust that God will interpret my thought to your heart in a more forceful manner than words will allow.

Thus far I have been speaking mainly to young workers in the early part of their ministry. Now I wish to say a few words that will be helpful to them as they grow older in the service. If you are fully persuaded that God has chosen you as his mouthpiece to declare the everlasting gospel to eternity-bound souls, you should feel the weight of your responsibility. A very weighty responsibility rests upon him who stands between the living and the dead. The attitude a minister holds, both toward his call also toward the Word of God, and also toward the people, is of vital importance. No better instruction to ministers has ever been given than that which Paul gave to Timothy: "I charge thee, therefore, before God, and the Lord Jesus Christ, who shall judge the quick and the dead at his appearing and his kingdom; preach the word; be instant in season, out of season; reprove, rebuke, exhort with all long-suffering, and doctrine. For the time will come when they will not endure sound doctrine; but after their own lusts shall they heap to themselves teachers, having itching ears" (2 Timothy 4:1-3).

The admonition to preach the word implies that what goes forth from the pulpit should be in harmony with the Scriptures, backed up by the Spirit of God. Do not give the people theories nor illustrate your speech by fabulous stories. Do not dwell too much with the surface problems of Christianity, but spend more time in leading the people to a deep heart-experience. If they get the inner man right its beauty will shine out through their entire being. In short, speak to the people the oracles of God, so that if they are at all susceptible to the truth, your speech will appeal to them as the

Word of God spoken through your lips of clay.

In preaching, guard against relating many touching incidents merely to work up the human sympathy. We have to deal with the hearts of men as well as with their minds and judgments. Any one that has a love for God's pure word will find in it a force and power that will have a good effect when it is presented in simple and plain language under the anointing of the Holy Spirit.

In preaching on some subjects, it is necessary to have a large number of texts, but ministers make a mistake who think that they must make every sermon a Bible-reading. The use of too many scriptures confuses the listeners; it is often better to concentrate the attention of the hearers on one text until its full meaning is mastered. At the proper time Bible-lessons are in order, but the admonition, "Preach the word," does not mean that you are to read a large number of scriptures, but merely that you should present the Word of God as paramount to everything else. The ministry of Babylon have fed their people with much worldliness mixed together with a small portion of the Word of God. For this reason God's people scattered in Babylon have not fared well. At meeting their intellects would be fed, but their souls would be starved.

You can not, however, feed others until your own soul is fed. This is done by searching the Scriptures and by praying much. If it is laid upon any one more than another to search the Scriptures, it is laid upon God's ministry, whom he has set apart to teach his Word and to feed his people. It is good to read God's Word slowly and carefully, to meditate upon it, to read it in different ways, by course, by subject. After reading a small portion, take time to dwell upon it, to pray over it, until it has become your own, not only as a possession of your mind, but also as a soul-experience.

If you depend thus upon the Spirit of the Lord, he will give you new messages for the people. God gives his ministers many things that are good to repeat again and again, especially to different audiences; but a repetition of old thoughts many times in the same congregation is too much like serving warmed-over food. It lacks appetizing qualities. Something fresh from the Spirit of the Lord will make the people hungry to hear more of the word, and will make the word charming to their souls. When the minister gets a message direct from the Spirit, then presents it under the anointing of the Spirit, it will have beauty, sweetness, and a freshness that no power of mere human words, no trick of oratory, nor beauty of illustration, can give. If you will bear this in mind and drink of the Spirit before you come before your congregation, give the Lord a chance to use you as an avenue through which to speak, you will be a success in your calling.

To be a New Testament minister, you must be able to exhibit at least some of the gifts of the Spirit.

These are yours by right of your calling. Paul says, "But rather that ye should prophesy." Without this special insight into the Scriptures and power to present them to others, you will not be able to fulfil your calling as a mouthpiece of the Spirit.

Before laying special stress on the gifts, however, you would do well to see that you are filled with the Spirit. Remember that the gifts are as the fruits and the Spirit as the tree. One who has not the Spirit can not bear the fruit. Do not try to substitute the gifts of the Spirit for spirituality. Covet earnestly the best gifts. Nevertheless, you should be careful that you do not try by your own human efforts to obtain the gifts, instead of earnestly seeking the Lord for their bestowal. By undue human efforts, many have obtained the manifestation of a false spirit, which they have placed on exhibition as the genuine.

Paul said to Timothy, "Be instant in season." To do this you must keep close in touch with the Lord and let him be your wisdom, yea, your all. Paul said further, "Be instant out of season." This expression has been puzzling to many young ministers. If you will watch to do good and to lift up Christ at every possible opportunity, your chance for doing good will increase. Sometimes there will seem to be no opportunity, no open door; then you must open the door yourself. Go in and do what you can for souls. Sometimes what you do will seem altogether out of season. Later, however, you may see that God's blessing was upon your labors and that some soul has received a benefit.

"Reprove, rebuke, exhort with all long-suffering and doctrine." In order to be able to do this according to the Word of God, you will have to live a life above reproach, or your rebukes and reproofs will come back upon your own head, when rebuking and reproving, long-suffering is very needful. As a rule, people will not take the truth all at once. Paul said to Timothy in another place, "Consider what I say, and the Lord give thee understanding in all things." With what carefulness a minister must speak when he comes in contact with those who have not yet fallen in love with the truth. One word spoken unwisely may forever shut the door of salvation for some eternity-bound soul.

The last word in this admonition should not be forgotten: "with all long-suffering and doctrine." Doctrine has a very important place. Mistakes have been made in preaching the Word. Sometimes it is all doctrine and no experience; sometimes it is all experience and no doctrine.

Paul said to Titus, "But speak thou the things which become sound doctrine." And to Timothy: "Till I come, give attendance to reading, to exhortation, to doctrine.... Take heed unto thyself, and unto the doctrine; continue in them, for in doing this thou shalt both save thyself and them that hear thee." Paul's words seem to show that the doctrines of the New Testament are of vital importance. For example, we should understand the doctrine of repentance and justification, of sanctification, of divine healing, of the one body, and of every other subject connected with our eternal interest. If a minister keeps the church well grounded in the doctrine of the New Testament, he will in a large measure forestall the possibility of their being seduced by false spirits and of giving place to doctrines of devils.

But to know the doctrine means more than to gain a mental knowledge of it. No minister is properly equipped to teach justification or sanctification until he has an actual heart-experience. As the minister presents the truth on these doctrines, the Spirit of the Lord should bear definite witness to his possession of these graces, so that he can present the truth definitely from an experimental standpoint. Then he will not say, "I think it is so and so," or "I guess it is this way or that," but he can speak with authority.

"Holding fast the faithful word as he hath been taught

that he may be able by sound doctrine, both to exhort and to convince the gainsayers" (Titus 1:9). God's Word on any point, illuminated by the Spirit, brings out sound doctrine. It is certain that we can not improve on the Word. We may give illustrations which are good in their place, but these can not improve on the Word. We may give illustrations which are good in their place, but these [words missing] of God's Spirit, knowing that we have the experience in ourselves, God can so impress our teachings upon our hearers that it will be difficult to ever get them mixed up in doctrine.

"Sound speech, that can not be condemned; that he that is of the contrary part may be ashamed, having no evil thing to say of you" (Titus 2:8). Our speech in the pulpit should be of such a nature that it will appeal to the hearers. Foolishness, lightness, jesting, indulged in by the minister while preaching the everlasting gospel, is entirely out of place. Nor does this admonition apply entirely to the pulpit, but at all times, under all circumstances, a minister should be an example to the flock. Only thus can we ministers expect to obey God and fulfil our calling and accomplish God's will in the salvation of the world.

Those who are young in the ministry should not get discouraged because they have not fully comprehended and practised the different things herein set forth. The older ministers should encourage the young to do all they know of God's will and to trust him to make his will plainer and clearer. Young minister, you should encourage yourself. You should be patient under the molding and fashioning hand of God, trusting him so to fasten these truths upon your heart and mind that it will be as natural to practise them as it is to breathe. If we as ministers are humble enough, God can get to the people through us what he wants the people to hear. If we would but be patient under God's controlling power and let him work out in us his own good pleasure, we should have less trouble and there would be fewer mistakes to be cleared up. Our lives should be living epistles, known and read of all men, so that when the world reads our lives, they will read the Bible.

It is very essential to the welfare of the minister as well as to the welfare of the church that the ministers treat each other with special courtesy and consideration. The mere act of a young minister in taking an easy seat and leaving some older brother or sister in the ministry to sit in an uncomfortable place, and other similar acts of discourtesy, will have a bad effect upon the congregation. Many times young ministers hold an irreverent attitude toward older ones. They should consider them as their seniors and as fathers in the gospel. Older ministers, too, should act as fathers in the gospel and show all consideration and kindness when giving advice and admonition to the younger brethren. Before approaching a younger worker to admonish or instruct him, you who are older in the gospel work, should wait carefully before God in prayer for what to say. You should call to mind the testings, trials, and experiences of your younger days in the ministry. If you keep these fully in mind and speak to the young ministers as you would have wished some one to speak to you in your early days, you can save your younger brethren in the ministry many heartaches and trials. If approached in this way, they are much more likely to heed your warnings and your advice.

Young people are apt to think that if a road appears fair before them it is safe to travel. Sometimes in the path that seems so open to you, the older ones see pitfalls and dangers. If you will but be cautioned by those who are more experienced, you will be saved many trials and heartaches. Again, young ministers are sometimes very timid and do not exercise themselves in spiritual things as they should, especially in the presence of their elders. When this occurs, both the older and younger ministers should do all they can to remedy the trouble. The older ministers should encourage the younger to do their duty, and the younger should lean on God for the help they need, and should move out, even when they have to go with fear and trembling.

Dear young fellow worker, if you want to make a success of your calling, keep close to the Savior; keep in touch with him at all times. Do not let your mind drift away on things that are not for your good. Let your meditation be such that your soul will be stored with truths that will be helpful to give out to others.

The subject of our thoughts has much to do with our speech and determines whether our words will be wholesome to present to the people. The apostle gives very definite instructions on this point. "Finally, brethren, whatsoever things are true, whatsoever things are honest, whatsoever things are just, whatsoever things are pure, whatsoever things are lovely, whatsoever things are of good report; if there be any virtue, and if there be any praise, think on these things" (Philemon 4:8). Let your mind dwell upon God, upon his plan, upon his goodness and his mercy, then the Lord will have a chance to impress these things upon your soul more clearly than they can be impressed in any other manner.

With your meditation, combine secret prayer. As you

meditate, talk with God and let God talk with you. To have a good conversation with a friend, you must not do all the talking, but must give your friend an opportunity to talk also. Likewise, when you are talking with God, give him a chance to reveal precious thoughts to your soul. Give him a chance to fill your inner being with heaven's sweetness. If God fills your heart with the riches of heaven, then you can give out that richness and blessing to others; then you can be the means of arousing in your hearers a hungering for the good things of God, and they will come again to hear the Word of the Lord.

Now, as I bring to a close this brief sketch of my life history, I realize that, like this story, my active work in the ministry is near its close. Although my body is well spent and the weight of years is somewhat heavy upon me, yet the divine fire still glows on the altar of my heart, and my interest in gospel work is not diminished. In the few years that may still remain to me of my earthly pilgrimage, I shall take a lively interest in those young brothers and sisters whom God has called to take the places of us who are being compelled to retire from active service.

I shall watch with interest the work of the ministry, not only as individuals but as a body. I shall hope and pray that you who are now stepping into the ranks as workers for the Lord will avoid many mistakes that we older ministers have made. If this little volume points out any pitfalls that should be avoided or any pleasant paths that your feet may walk in with safety; if it encourages you to trust the Lord more fully for all things and inspire you to place yourself more fully in his hands for service, it will have accomplished the purpose of the author.

Our salvation was purchased by the suffering and death of Christ. The salvation of the world will be brought about only through our suffering and soul-travail. "They that sow in tears shall reap in joy." "As soon as Zion travailed, she brought forth her children." "He that goeth forth and weepeth, bearing precious seed, shall doubtless come again with rejoicing, bringing his sheaves with him."

Remember that without trials you can not have triumphs. Paul says something about enduring hardness like good soldiers, thus recognizing the fact that hardness is the portion of a good soldier. If you are a worthy minister, you are sure to endure hardness, buffeting, persecution, and perils by false brethren; but, thank God, through all these you can be more than conqueror, and look forward to the final reward. Paul says, "I reckon that the sufferings of this present time are not worthy to be compared with the glory that shall be revealed in us."

THE REFINER'S FIRE

He sat by a fire of seven-fold heat,
As he watched by the precious ore,
And closer He bent with a searching gaze
As he heated it more and more.

He knew he had ore that could stand the test,
And he wanted the finest gold
To mold as a crown for the King to wear,
Set with gems with a price untold.

So he laid our gold in the burning fire,
Though we fain would have said him "Nay,"
And he watched the dross that we had not seen,
And it melted and passed away.

And the gold grew brighter and yet more bright,
But our eyes were so dim with tears,
We saw but the fire, not the Master's hand,
And questioned with anxious fears.

Yet our gold shone out with a richer glow,
As it mirrored a Form above,
That bent o'er the fire, though unseen by us,
With a look of ineffable love.

Can we think that it pleases His loving heart
To cause us a moment's pain?

Ah, no! but He saw through the present cross
The bliss of eternal gain.

So He waited there with a watchful eye,
With a love that is strong and sure,
And His gold did not suffer a whit more heat

Mary Cole